The Psychic Cop

The Psychic Cop

Chuck Bergman

BALBOA.
PRESS

A DIVISION OF HAY HOUSE

ISBN: 978-1-4525-5144-9 (sc)
ISBN: 978-1-4525-5143-2 (e)

Library of Congress Control Number: 2012907985

Balboa Press books may be ordered through booksellers or by contacting:

Balboa Press
A Division of Hay House
1663 Liberty Drive
Bloomington, IN 47403
www.balboapress.com
1-(877) 407-4847

Because of the dynamic nature of the Internet, any web addresses or links contained in this book may have changed since publication and may no longer be valid. The views expressed in this work are solely those of the author and do not necessarily reflect the views of the publisher, and the publisher hereby disclaims any responsibility for them.

The author of this book does not dispense medical advice or prescribe the use of any technique as a form of treatment for physical, emotional, or medical problems without the advice of a physician, either directly or indirectly. The intent of the author is only to offer information of a general nature to help you in your quest for emotional and spiritual well-being. In the event you use any of the information in this book for yourself, which is your constitutional right, the author and the publisher assume no responsibility for your actions.

Any people depicted in stock imagery provided by Thinkstock are models, and such images are being used for illustrative purposes only.
Certain stock imagery © Thinkstock.

Printed in the United States of America

Balboa Press rev. date: 5/4/2012

To Sharon Merrill, my best friend, you add "class" to everything you do. Thank you. Cheers!

Chuck Bergman is the ultimate hero! Not only did he protect and serve as a police officer for over thirty years, his God-given talent as a psychic medium now helps countless people around the world solve the mysteries behind their loved ones' passing and or disappearances. Chuck's background in law enforcement, and the ability to see and speak to the other side, makes him the most unique and sought after psychic medium of our time.

David Tadman
Writer and Producer

For anyone who has wondered where our loved ones go after death, Chuck will answer your question. He has received the most remarkable gift of being able to communicate with the other side. Chuck's compassion, wisdom and calming nature enables his clients to feel comfortable and at ease, as he passes along incredibly accurate and personal information. Chuck reinforces the hope that our departed loved ones are always around us, and that the spirit lives on.

Robert Arena
Clerk Magistrate, (Ret.) Essex County, MA.

The Psychic Cop takes the reader into the world of one of America's renowned mediums, Chuck Bergman. This book reveals his personal experiences from the moment of discovering he had the ability to communicate with spirits through the process of developing that gift. Chuck's mediumship work with clients makes for fascinating reading and, more importantly, validates life after death

.

Alison Baughman
Numerologist, Radio Host, Pennsylvania
www.visiblebynumbers.com

A close friend, who had recently lost her husband, referred us to Chuck when our 30-year-old son suddenly passed away. Chuck connected us with Sean, whose sense of humor and personality came through loud and clear. We learned that he was happy and safe where he was, and that he was watching over us. The grief and loss that was taken away after Chuck's reading made it possible for us to live a normal life again. We can't thank him enough for his help.

John and Karen Edgar
Parents

Born With a Gift

Early Signs

Like most young children, I was afraid of the dark. There were scary figures hiding in the closet. I would hear movement under the bed and imagine all kinds of spooky things. My older brother, Fred, loved to further terrorize me with his many antics at bedtime. I always felt that these fears were real and that there were people hiding in my room. I recall seeing dark shadowy images moving around with no distinct features.

At the age of five, my grandmother, who lived in Wales, came to see us in Florida. On the first night of her visit, I was awakened and frightened by a group of people standing around my bed, looking down at me. I could hear them talking, but I couldn't understand what they were saying. They spoke too quickly; it was like listening to a radio that was not properly tuned. It was like looking at real people in a darkened room. I clearly recall recognizing heights of each individual. It was easy to distinguish male from female.

My grandmother was watching television and came into my room when she heard me scream. She took me with her into the living room to comfort me. A late night movie was starting, and she told me that I could watch it with her. A few minutes into the movie, she slyly asked me why I was frightened. I told her about the figures standing around my bed, looking down at me. She then asked me how many figures and if I could describe them. As I did so, she let me know that she knew each of the apparitions. She told me, "I knew one of the grandchildren would have this ability. Chucky, you are very special to have this gift." Throughout her visit, I carefully listened to see if she told my other brothers and sisters that they, too, were special.

I didn't learn until much later in life that both my grandmother and mother were gifted in the same way. They quietly shared their abilities with their closest friends. Acceptance at that time was not like it is today.

About a year after the incident with my grandmother, I recall playing alone in my backyard, pretending to be a policeman. I sculpted a police badge out of aluminum foil, but got very frustrated and started to cry when I could not get it to stay on my shirt. I then heard a man's calming voice say, *That's okay Chuck; one day you'll wear a real badge.* The voice was not one that I could recognize. He sounded crystal clear, just like a radio announcer. I ran into the house, afraid to tell my mom for fear that she would not believe me.

Twenty years later I was standing before the Mayor of the City of Salem, Massachusetts while he pinned a real badge on my chest. I, admittedly, had a flashback of my childhood and the tin badge. With all the major undertakings in my life, I've only heard that voice several times. Usually it will speak to me when I'm deep in thought or contemplating a major decision.

Mom was a Medium

At dinner one night, my mother let out a gasp and buckled to the floor, holding her chest, saying, "My heart, my heart." Dad called for an ambulance, and as mom recovered herself, she started crying and said, "It's not me, it's my dad." My grandfather had died at that exact time, halfway around the world, in Wales.

Dad never talked about the afterlife. He was of a manly world, and the display of feelings and tears were not manly. I've always felt that he was harder on me than he was on my siblings because I was so sensitive.

After surgery for an appendectomy, I was awakened in my hospital room and saw my mother standing at the foot of the bed. Her arms were outstretched with palms up and her head tilted back. I saw a beautiful bright, white light silhouetting her entire body. I called out to my mom and asked what she was doing. I remember her saying that she was praying for me to get well. When I asked about the white light, she did not answer.

Then, as in later years, she seemed not to want me to continue on this path. Paranormal things would happen around me, and I would have premonitions that would later come to fruition. In those instances, mom would make light of the matter and claim that it was simply my imagination. Her choice was to keep her abilities private for the same reason she wanted to discount mine; she feared our gift would be ridiculed.

Fascinated with Communications

I have always had an interest in communications. Around age ten, I was intrigued by the concept of a radio antenna sending out voice and music through the airways without wires. I remember taking apart my dad's favorite table-top AM radio and removing parts from the tuning device. I was able to hear strange transmissions such as ship-to-shore radio and other broadcasts not normally picked up by AM radio.

I was hoping to go beyond standard broadcast frequencies and discover that there really is other life form out there. I would spend hours listening to white noise and would hear fragments of voices where there should have been none. In later years, my fascination with communication led me to earning an amateur radio technician's license with the FCC.

Studying for a ham license required learning Morse code at a rate of five words per minute. The code consists of a series of audible dots and dashes that represent the alphabet. A seasoned ham operator can communicate at over thirty words per minute. Nick, a neighbor and friend of mine, whose "keying" speed was around fifty words per minute, communicated with contacts around the world on a regular schedule.

Nick had a brother living in Ireland with whom he spoke every day using code. The cost of conventional phone service would have been prohibitive. To my untrained ear, it sounded like a series of meaningless pitches and tones. To Nick and his brother, it was a normal conversation.

Nick could simultaneously talk with me while hearing and interpreting the faint radio messages in the background.

Spirit communication can require the same concentration as hearing Morse code. Words can be very fast to the untrained ear. With practice, the messages are more easily understood. The communication goes better if you are on a regular schedule with spirit. They look for opportunities to connect with us. When a reading is scheduled, they almost always show up, as if they were anticipating it.

Anchors Aweigh

During my last year of high school, the Vietnam War was going strong. My older brother joined the Navy, and I was struggling just to stay in school. One night I had a vivid dream that I was standing in front of three red brick buildings. I recall seeing the American flag. The sun was just coming up, but it was very hot in the dream. I was standing in the front row of a military inspection, and the Sergeant was in my face. I awoke after he screamed at me for not shaving close enough. I was sweating, and the dream seemed quite real. I went into my mother's bedroom and told her what had happened. As usual, she said that it was just a dream and to go back to sleep.

Even though I had no thoughts of going into the Navy, one month later I found myself standing in the front row facing that same Drill Sergeant, surrounded by those same red brick buildings and the American flag. It was hot at boot camp in Orlando, FL. I was in the Navy now! My hand was shaking as I wrote a letter to my mother that afternoon telling her that the dream had played out exactly as I had experienced it. Mom never did reply to that letter.

After boot camp, I was assigned to the aircraft carrier Shangri La, the same ship on which my brother was currently serving. Our home port of Mayport was in our home town of Jacksonville. Life on board an aircraft carrier while at sea can be very boring at times. Watch stations should provide a perfect opportunity to put yourself in a meditative state, even though you have not been exposed to the process. You sit for hours with nothing to do. Your one task is to stay awake. During those duties, I never experienced any spirit communication. My surroundings would have provided a perfect opportunity for it. Between my Navy career and early police years, it seems I entered a time of "intermission" from the spirit world.

It's All Coming Back to Me Now

Boston

After I returned from Vietnam, the aircraft carrier was sent to Boston to be decommissioned. Within a few days of arriving in Boston, three other sailors and I started out early one morning to tour the New England area. That evening, we pulled into a rest stop in a very small town and ended up sleeping in the car all night.

The next day we toured the seaport of Manchester-by-the-Sea. While working our way back to the base, we entered the City of Salem. Although I had never been there before, buildings and street names looked familiar to me. I was literally telling the other guys what to expect around the next corner, and I was accurate each time.

Two months later, I met a woman who was going to nursing school near the Navy base. After a few dates, we drove to her hometown of Manchester-by-the-Sea. While spending the weekend at her parents' house, they asked me how I had slept in the guest room. I was reluctant to tell them that during the night, I saw a very small man dressed in a tuxedo. Her dad told me that their house, at one time, had been a Masonic Temple, and that the Masons always dressed in tuxedos. Her dad said, "Now that makes sense." He told me that while redoing the guest room, he found traces of wallpaper with the Masonic logo. The house was three hundred years' old.

At the end of my tour in the Navy, I married the nurse, and we purchased a home in Salem MA. A close friend of mine introduced me to ambulance work. This set the stage for my EMT training and taking the Civil Service exam to become a police officer.

It felt so right when I was in City Hall, having the badge pinned on for the first time. I remembered my childhood experience of the toy badge and the voice saying, *One day you will have a real badge.* This badge stayed on for 32 years.

Haunted Hotel

It was common for me to leave the cold weather in New England and vacation with family in Florida. My brother, Roger, was a manager of a well-known hotel on Jacksonville Beach. He invited my family to stay at the hotel for a few days, and we were delighted.

The first night, I joined Roger in the bar for a drink, and he told me the story about the ghost on the second floor. A "lady of the night" had been violently murdered in one of the rooms on the second floor within the last year.

Roger said that they had totally remodeled the room, and even businessmen refused to spend an entire night there because of visits from the ghost. With time, it was reported that she would roam the hallway and visit every room on the second floor, frightening the guests. Management found it necessary to close off the entire second floor. My brother-in-law, Don, who was also staying at the hotel said, "Where is this room? I'll sleep there tonight."

We went up to the closed floor, as I wanted to test my psychic abilities. I wanted to prove to the others that I could identify the room where the murder had happened. I walked down the hallway, touching every door, hoping to get a sense of the murder scene.

The final door was room number 205. As I approached to place my hand on that door, my knees got weak, and I felt nauseated. I emphatically stated, "This is where it happened, this is where it happened."

Roger's facial expression told me that I was right. I had to go in, but the door was locked. Roger said that he would get the master key. As we walked toward the office, we heard a loud crash that sounded like someone kicking in a door. We turned and went back to room 205 to find the door standing wide open.

We went inside and talked for a few minutes. Roger then held up his arm, grinning, and said, "Look, she's here." The hair on his arm was standing straight up. He said, "She does this all the time." Roger turned on the cable TV, which started off with a clear picture that quickly turned to snow. I called up to my wife on the fifth floor and asked her to turn on the same channel. She said the picture was perfect.

A year later, I visited Florida and saw a newscast announcing that the suspect in the hotel murder had been found guilty. I felt a need to return to room 205 and read the verdict out loud. I met there with Roger and did so. After this was done, we felt a sense of relief and peace. There was no longer paranormal activity in the room.

They're Back

Life was rolling on with little or no spirit contact. I was preoccupied with police work and raising two daughters. Several years passed, and then while returning home from a Christmas shopping trip in New Hampshire with my wife, I felt the presence of an older lady who had just passed over. I asked my wife the time. She said, "2:30." She could tell that I looked puzzled and asked me what was going on. I told her about the presence of the older lady. I could tell that she was not a family member and that her passing was very peaceful. Her reason for appearing was to say "Thank you" to my wife. Upon returning home, we had a voice message time-stamped at 2:30 p.m. from my wife's closest friend. She stated that her mother had just passed away and that my wife was not needed the following day to take care of her mom, as planned. This was the first time in several years that such a message was given to me.

A few days later, I was awakened at 4:00 in the morning by the spirit of an older male known to me. He told me that he had just died but was okay now. My energy level was so elevated that I could not go back to sleep. Fortunately, I relayed this information to my wife, at which time she went back to sleep.

At 7:00 a.m. my wife's co-worker friend called to say that her dad had just suffered a heart attack and had stopped breathing; she resuscitated him with CPR, and he was now in ICU. Perhaps his connection with me was that we worked together on a video the previous week. I wondered why he had come to me in spirit, as we never discussed my interest in the afterlife, and he had never been to my house. This did get my wife's attention, but she was never supportive of my psychic ability.

Several months later, while awakening from sleep, I heard a male voice speak the words, "plane crash." My wife was preparing to fly to California to visit with family. My first impulse was to wake her and tell her to reschedule her flight. I decided not to frighten her and carefully considered what I had heard.

As I would do every morning, I went upstairs, showered, shaved, and put on the local radio broadcast. I listened to details of a plane crash. It was TWA flight 800, down on July 17, 1996. I had to weigh out whether the message that I had heard was a warning for my wife not to take her flight or a message of the actual plane crash that had just occurred. She took her scheduled flight without incident.

When a major traumatic event is about to happen, the spirit world is preparing for the new arrivals, creating an upsurge of communication. Many psychics are made aware of disasters by sensing the extra activity and tapping into an incident which has already occurred or is about to happen.

Meditation

Later the following year, I went to Florida to stay at my sister's lake house with a fellow officer for a short vacation. My cousin, Yvonne, whom I had never met, was flying over from England to also vacation at the lake house.

Yvonne had already written a book on spiritualism and taught mediumship in England. The first night, Yvonne offered to conduct a meditation session for our small group. My understanding of a meditation at the time was that it was simply a way to clear the mind and make a person feel relaxed.

She gave a guided meditation without music. All we had to do was close our eyes and listen to her words. When it was over, she asked me if I saw anything. I told her that I felt like I was standing in a small, extremely messy, bedroom. An older woman was pointing to a lamp on the top of a dresser, and I was amazed at how brilliantly green the lamp shade was. Yvonne told me that her next door neighbor, who was like a grandmother, had died within the last few months. Her room was, indeed, very small and messy, and Yvonne had given her the lamp with the green shade.

I still felt confused the next day, and I even considered that I had been hypnotized or, better yet, that one big joke had been played on me. Late that afternoon, we did another meditation. I closed my eyes and, at first, could only see darkness. Then I saw coming from just above my eyebrow area, about five inches outward, a cream-colored round disc the size of a quarter. It was moving downward at a very slow rate. I asked my cousin why I would be seeing this; she seemed to already know what was going on and advised me to just keep watching it and report on its location. After about three minutes' time, the disc was in front of me at the same distance. I felt as if I could literally pluck it out of the air. The descent rate was constant, and after a few more minutes, the disc disappeared below me. When I lost sight of it, I let her know. Shortly after, the same disc appeared on the right side of my field of vision. It traveled at the same rate of speed from my right side to my left until it was out of sight, which took approximately five to six minutes. I learned later that this was done by my spirit guides in order to assess my visual range for future images they wished to show me.

During this same visit, and in another meditation with Yvonne and our group, I had a direct voice experience. Yvonne was, again, giving a guided meditation. I then heard a male voice say, *Chuck, say Ha, Ha, Ha.* I mentally responded that I would not, as I didn't want to disrupt the meditation for the others. He repeated it again quite sternly and loud. I told him, "I won't do it, but you can do it." He said, *You have to move over,* and I didn't know what that meant. I opened my eyes and asked Yvonne the meaning. She smiled and said, "I can see you've been reading up on this stuff." She said that "moving over" would be like moving my spirit to the side of my body allowing room for the other entity to make use of my body, especially my vocal cords.

"The reason he wanted you to say "Ha, Ha, Ha" was so that he could continue the vibration of the last "Ha" in the hopes of making it into a word or sentence." Because I broke continuity with him, all I was able to do was break out into a laugh not my own. The pitch and sound were ones Yvonne recognized from her past.

Eager for Information

Upon my return from Florida, I was still mystified as I realized that I had the ability to communicate with the spirit world. I was eager for information and now knew there were groups out there from whom I could learn much more. Many of my closest friends would not carry on a conversation that had anything to do with the afterlife. I had reached a point of asking myself, "Do I give this up, or do I pursue it?"

I booked my first reading with a medium in a small angel shop in Salem, MA. The medium's name was Barbara Szafranski, and the shop was called "Angelica of the Angels." This was not a likely place for a motorcycle cop to walk into. My intent was to find out more about my experiences in Florida and why I got the message of the plane crash. The medium told me that when there is a major catastrophe, word is sent out to angels, healers and other sensitives.

She told me that I was developing my skills as a medium, and I had to think of myself as being like an antenna receiving messages on an improperly tuned radio. I would have to learn to interpret the meanings, and I am still doing that today.

While I trusted her information, she added that my mother was standing next to me in spirit. She told me that she could hear my mom speak and loved her British accent! She further stated, "Your mom has her hands extended out, palms up, holding a very small gift-wrapped package with a bow on it." The day of the reading was actually on my birthday.

I was craving more information on spirit communication. I wanted all of this to be real, that we don't die, and that communication is possible. The medium recommended that I attend meditation classes in her shop. I started immediately. In the first class I attended, I was the only male present and felt very out of place. It didn't help that the shop was full of angels, fairies and crystals; all things from a world unfamiliar to me. My world consisted of guns, handcuffs, and billy clubs.

We were given brief instructions on how to meditate. The music started, and in a flash, it was over. I remember feeling that I had knowledge somewhere in my brain, but was not sure how it got there or what it was. The protocol was to go around the room and let each person share his or her experience of the meditation.

When it came to me, I don't know what made me do it, but I stood up, turned to the lady next to me and asked her to stand. I gave her a hug, which was totally out of character for me. I proceeded to tell her that I had a visit from a twenty-five-year-old female named Gail. I described her as very thin, long brown hair, and pretty. Gail told me that she had died in a car accident and had a message for the woman I was speaking to. The message was, *I will be there.* The woman informed me that I had described her daughter, Gail, who had died at the age of twenty five in a car accident. She further told me that Gail's daughter, her granddaughter, would be getting married next month. Gail wanted mom and her daughter to know that she would "be there" at the wedding. Mom had come to the meditation in hopes of receiving such a message.

Silver Cord

In the metaphysical world, silver cord refers to a life-giving link from the higher self to the physical body. It connects the physical body to the etheric body. The silver cord is mentioned in many near-death experiences. If the silver cord is entirely severed, the spirit is out of this earthly plane. I had heard the term "silver cord" but had no idea what it meant.

One of the meditation classes I attended was located on a very busy four-lane highway. The house was only 200 feet from the road. The instructor felt that achieving a meditative state with the distraction of the traffic noise was the ultimate test of concentration.

One morning, we began the meditation, and within minutes I found myself standing in the high- speed lane of the road outside. The sensation was strange, especially when cars and trucks whizzed through my body without pain or consequence. For a brief moment, I could see what was in the cars as they passed through. This went on for a couple of minutes, and then I saw a large tractor-trailer truck barreling down on me. As I looked through the windshield at the driver, he stared back, startled, as if he could see me. I didn't quite understand that this was a part of my meditation; it felt very real. I wasn't sure if I could quickly return to the house for safety. As I turned my head to look in the direction of the house, I saw a silver cable which looked like an umbilical cord. It was puckered and wrinkled but continuously attached to my belly button and floated into the house where my body was seated. I looked up at the truck, and the next thing I knew, I was sitting in front of the others in the group looking very startled.

After meditation, it is common practice to go around the circle and let each person tell of their individual experience during the session. At my turn, I started telling the story about being out in the highway traffic and what it felt like. I remembered seeing the silver cord. I asked the instructor, "By the way, what was this cord attached to me?"

Barbara said, "Chuck, that's the silver cord; don't you know about it?

I said, "No." She continued to explain it to me. I was, obviously, still on my learning curve.

Salem Spiritualist Church

A good friend of mine lived on a quiet residential street in Salem, and on one corner was a small Spiritualist Church. As we walked by, he told me that strange people went there and talked to the dead. This made me pay attention and read the marquee to learn about the next service.

The following Sunday, I attended the church service. Entering the church was very intimidating to me. I wondered why I was doing this. To my surprise, people were friendly; they all seemed to know each other. It began with a regular prayer service followed by a hands-on healing session. I went up to the front to let them do a healing on me so that I would appear to blend in with the people. A woman medium stood at the podium and started giving messages to people in the congregation. Most people understood their messages which were rather quick and to the point.

The medium singled me out and told me that my dad was standing next to me. "He's showing me an alligator with his tail curled up."

I said, "My dad died in Florida," as the others chuckled.

She said, "He's very rugged, but I don't understand why he's posing the way he is." She mimicked what she was seeing, with both arms by her side, fists clenched approximately one foot away from her body. My dad worked for a dairy and used to carry wooden milk crates containing nine half-gallons of milk in each hand. I knew what the pose represented as soon as I saw her do it. She further said, "Your dad was with you when you were playing the same song over and over." That afternoon, I had spent many hours putting music to wedding pictures I was editing on my computer. Each time a few pictures were added, I would have to repeat playback to make sure that the music and pictures flowed together.

Near the end of the service, six graduating students of the mediumship class offered at the church were waiting on the pulpit to give readings to the congregation. This was their final exam to determine whether or not each was ready to go out and give readings accurately to the public.

I was impressed with the style and accuracy of the five girls as they took turns giving messages. They named family members in spirit by name and gave several other validations that left the audience laughing, or gasping for air, in surprise. The last in the group to address the audience was David. He was much older than the girls and had been a Spiritualist for many years, practicing as a healer.

David walked to the center stage and immediately made it clear that he was a healer not a medium. He drew in a deep breath, closed his eyes and tilted his head back. After thirty seconds of this, his hands which were at his side floated slightly away from his body, and he turned his palms upward. He stood before us for several minutes hoping to get just one message that would confirm his achievement of becoming a medium.

Finally, he tilted his head forward and slowly opened his eyes. He looked from side to side. He stared at me for a moment. My hopes were up that I would get a message from a loved one. He then closed his eyes again.

David was breathing in slowly and exhaling, but nothing was happening. He continued focusing for fifteen minutes and finally gave up. He said, "I've been given the gift of healing, and I still have that gift. Some of you are given the gift of mediumship. You must be honest and only give out what you receive. It is now clear to me that I am a healer and not a medium. Today my job was to show you how hard it is to do what you do."

David has been an inspiration to me, and I have never had the opportunity to express my gratitude to him. He gave it his best shot and then conceded to continue doing what he did best.

Swampscott Church of Spiritualism

After going to the Salem church on a regular basis, I learned of a larger spiritualist church in the next community of Swampscott. I attended their services because I liked the meditations they offered. They would have mediums from around the country, as well as from around the world. The messages were powerful and a good part of the service. I used these experiences as a large part of my learning platform.

After the services, classes were offered for aspiring mediums. The focus was to teach us to overcome stage fright and still stay connected to our sources on the other side. I found myself getting on stage, but I had to be the last. I was simply afraid of getting up in front of the group. I wanted to see how the others who went before me did. I secretly knew that if they bombed, or fell short on their readings, I wouldn't look so bad if I failed.

After a few months, I reached the point where I knew that stage fright was holding me back. I decided that the next time the instructor asked for someone to go on stage, I would go first. My attitude was that it didn't matter if I gave a good reading or not. I just had to overcome the fear. My next time, I gave a very good reading and was first up for the following three weeks. With practice, I got quite comfortable with group sessions.

The church was grooming several of us for an evening of readings which was open to the public.

Only three would be performing on stage. After several months of practice, two other women and I were selected from our group. The night of the event, there was standing room only, and I was a bit intimidated. The three mediums were sitting at the rear of the stage while the instructor explained the protocol. In this case, I was the last to give readings. When it was my turn to give messages, I stepped out, looked around the group and had no clue as to what to say. This was the worst feeling, and I started to doubt my abilities, once again.

I took a deep breath, pointed to the rear of the room and said, "I want to talk to a person in the last row on the right, and I'm hearing the name "Parker." Does anyone associate with that name?" There was dead silence. I repeated the question a second time. There was total silence. I was frustrated; I felt like a magnet had pulled me to the right side and last row. I knew that I had heard the name "Parker."

I used what I called distraction techniques to bring my energy to the opposite side of the room. I pointed to a male and gave him a fifteen minute reading that was complicated and completely accurate. I moved on to several other people with the same success.

When the event ended, we were gathered for refreshments to give the audience a chance to mingle with the mediums. I recall an elderly, small man approaching me. He put his hand out to shake and said, "Mr. Bergman, that was really interesting, but I would like to ask you a question. When you singled out the last row on the right and said the name "Parker," my name is "Parker," but I was in next to the last row. Should I have raised my hand?" I could have punched him. I asked him if he knew an older woman who would have been small in stature and had passed within the last month. He stated that I was describing his wife. All I could do was shake my head and let him know that he had missed out on a message from her, and had made a fool of me at the same time.

This was a powerful message for me. Spirit communication is a three-way proposition --spirit, medium, and sitter. All three must work together. The more open and receptive the sitter is, the more effective and successful the reading will be.

Psychic Fair

Another thing I couldn't see myself doing was a psychic fair. But I did one. I was invited by a friend to the event. It was in his hometown which was an hour and a half away, and I felt I could go there incognito. I wasn't ready for fellow officers to see me giving readings near my own home town. The setting was in a church which had many tables set up for individual readings. The tables were placed in a large, open room. I did not feel comfortable with this arrangement, because there was no privacy and many distractions. I could easily hear others giving their readings. I was afraid I wouldn't be able to concentrate.

My first reading was for a woman who had lost her son to a car accident. I described the scene of the accident and his position in the car. I told her that he was sitting in the back seat and had died from the seatbelt rupturing his stomach. The woman informed me that her husband was waiting outside in the car and had sent her in to see if the mediums were any good. He wanted to connect with his son, but wanted his wife to test the water. We took a short break so that she could go outside to get her husband. The reading for the couple went on for about an hour.

When we said our goodbyes, I learned that word had already traveled, and I had a line of about twenty people waiting to sit with me. Many in the open room had heard my validations and passed the word on to others. My energy was totally drained, as I had been working nonstop since 10:00 a.m. that morning. However, I felt I could not refuse the eager others and continued with my readings until 6:00 p.m. that evening.

The psychic fair did build my confidence, and I started doing private readings in my home. All my customers were from word of mouth. The excitement of giving a reading and learning that the information was accurate carried into my workplace. I started sharing some of my stories with a select few co-workers. Their responses were mixed.

Meeting James Van Praagh

No Turning Back

In the Salem Police Department, I was assigned to Special Operations with the duties of Accident Reconstructionist. I was also the department's computer specialist. I dealt with facts and concrete evidence in a black and white world. Like reconstructing a fatal accident, I would piece together bits of information from the spirit world, which could be validated, to support the fact that life continues after death. It took me several years to finally accept that spirit communication was real despite my success with private readings. If I felt this way, how could I expect my peers to have an open mind or a belief in the afterlife?

A female officer in my division stopped by my office and asked me if I would like to have a book written by James Van Praagh entitled, "Talking to Heaven." Someone had given it to her after her father had died two months earlier. She attempted to read the book, but felt that it was eerie. I accepted the book and read it within two days. For me to read a book in two days is a rarity. I was incredibly impressed with it.

Within a few days, I learned of a book signing with James Van Praagh at a nearby bookstore in Peabody, MA. I attended the event and was surprised by the number of people who had come out in a snowstorm to meet him. James did his opening speech, which took longer than expected. He stated that he was running late for the airport and would not be able to personalize books, only to quickly sign them.

As he signed my book, he looked up and said to me, "My mother in spirit is talking to your mother in spirit. Why aren't you doing what I'm doing?" I let him know that I wanted to do readings and further my education in this field. He offered me information on how I could go to his website to network with other people with the same interests.

James was one of the first to utilize chat room technology on a website. This allowed people with similar interests in the spirit world, and those grieving for their loved ones, to come together. On occasion, James would enter the chat room and give random readings to those present.

One evening, I was lucky enough to be the recipient of one of his readings. He started off by stating that he could feel a strong male presence around him. Things went downhill from there. He gave me about thirty five descriptions and statements about my dad; none made any sense at all.

The next morning at work, the officer who had given me the book entered my office and started reading my notes from the chat session. She identified every statement as being accurate, as they related to her dad. I felt things had gone full circle. She gave me the book, I met James, and he gave me the reading. Because she felt it was eerie in the first place, the message needed to come through me back to her.

James offered me a second reading thinking that he had failed on my behalf when, in fact, he was right on target for my co-worker. I was able to contact him the following day to express the peace and comfort his messages had brought to her. However, I never did get my second reading.

First Phone Reading

Later that year, my sister, Linda, from Florida called and asked me if I could "do that thing I do" over the telephone. I said, "I don't know, I've never tried, but on TV there are a lot of advertisements for phone readings." Coincidentally, James Van Praagh had called me asking me to do a reading for him. He needed to verify my credibility in order to include me on his practitioners' page. I had been very active in the JVP chat room, and word was traveling of my success. I thought this was a perfect opportunity to practice my first telephone reading with my sister, as I had just seven days before giving one to James.

Linda told me that her best friend had just passed. I asked, "Is her name Hilda? She is showing me a blue pickup truck." The name was correct, and Hilda had just purchased a new blue truck that she was bragging about to everyone. I further identified her actual cause of death. I started to feel good about my abilities on the telephone at that point.

I called many of my friends for free phone readings so that I could hone my gift. Even though these readings gave me more confidence, I was still nervous as hell about the upcoming one with James Van Praagh.

The reading for James took place on a Sunday afternoon. After he rescheduled two times, we were finally ready to go. He could tell that I was nervous and told me that it was no different giving him a reading than anyone else. My answer was that none of the other people I had practiced on had been on Hollywood Squares, like he had, the night before.

The session started out with his mom coming through in spirit. She showed me James exiting the back door of his house, turning to the right, and looking at his flower garden. She said, *James, the daisies are beautiful.*

I asked, "Did this happen when mom was alive?" James said, "No, it didn't." I was getting my payback. He offered that earlier in the day, he went out his back door, turned to the right, and planted a row of daisies. He then looked up to heaven and asked his mom, "How do you like the daisies? She never did answer," James said. "She knows I can do this; why did the answer have to come from you?" Mediums receive more accurate information when they have no personal relationship involved.

Fortunately for me, James Van Praagh has included me on his practitioners' page, which has connected me with a variety of people from around the world. Every reading is different. Some are uplifting, and some are tragic and sad. In all cases, I feel fortunate that I get to be the voice for those who can no longer speak. It is my mission to bring comfort to those grieving and to give affirmation that there is an afterlife.

James Van Praagh in Boston

James Van Praagh was doing a seminar in Boston, and I planned to attend. Jennifer, a member of the meditation group that I had joined, was also going. Boston was 30 miles away, and parking was scarce, so we shared the ride. I remember stopping for coffee and feeling the excitement about the eight-hour intensive event. I told Jennifer about meeting James at the book signing and about my reading with him. My hope was that he would remember me.

When we arrived at the First Baptist Church of Boston, the line was already wrapped around the building. As we inched slowly to the entrance, many people around us were telling stories about readings they had and how much comfort they found in them.

The show had sold out; the only seating available was in the balcony. James was introduced, and he walked out to the front edge of the stage.

"It's nice to be here in Boston again," he greeted us. He looked around the room at all the people.

"I was doing a meditation backstage, and my mother told me that Chuck, the Salem cop, was here; where are you Chuck?" I stood and said hello.

James started with a Q&A session. Many of the questions had to do with how spirits communicated and how James would see and hear the messages. I recall that one lady on the opposite balcony asked about her deceased husband and wanted to know why he hadn't come to her in a dream or in any other way. Teasingly, James said, "Maybe he doesn't want to talk to you." The lady sat down. After several similar questions, James started to do random readings.

The first reading started, and James pointed to the balcony across from me and said, "I'm hearing the name Becker."

The lady who had asked the question about not hearing from her husband stood and said, "My last name is Becker."

James said, "Your husband is here, and he wants to be the first to talk." This brought laughter to the audience.

Her husband gave accurate validations for 15 minutes. I was briefly distracted by the image of a motorcycle accident, as if it had just happened outside the church. James was finishing up the session with Mrs. Becker and had moved on to another person in the audience. He stopped, looked back at Mrs. Becker and said, "You're going on a cruise." Many psychics will see water or talk about a cruise, so I felt this was a cheesy thing to say after such an accurate reading.

"Yes, she replied, I'm leaving next week."

James was quiet for a moment and said, "You're going because of him?"

"Yes, I'm taking his ashes; he wanted to be buried at sea."

I felt guilty for thinking that the added piece of information was tacky. I've since learned to trust and to give out whatever message I receive. I should have known that James knew what he was doing.

Around noon, we took a break. Jennifer and I were having lunch with friends of ours, and I had another flash vision of a motorcycle accident. I didn't say anything because traffic around us was heavy, but flowing. There was no sign of an accident. We returned to the church for the second half of the show.

James did a guided meditation with the audience. When it ended, he selected individuals to talk about what they had experienced. People who had never done a meditation before were seeing spirits for the first time and found that the person standing next to them would recognize the name or description of the individual they had seen.

James ended the meditation show-and-tell part and was moving on to another aspect of the event. He stopped, looked up at me and said, "Chuck, what did you get?"

I stood and leaned over the balcony. "I have a message for someone sitting below me." I pointed to a family and said, "I keep seeing a motorcycle accident with a young man."

The father responded, "Our son died in a motorcycle accident."

I continued, "I'm seeing a blue and white motorcycle, and the young man is wearing a leather jacket that matches the colors of the bike. He is proudly holding his crash helmet over his head like a trophy. He wants me to see it. It also matches the jacket and bike."

The mother stated that he did, in fact, have a blue and white motorcycle, and the leather jacket matched. She had spent months finding a helmet that matched both and had given it to him as a graduation present.

I asked her if her son's name was "Nicky."

She said, "No, he was riding with his cousin Nicholas."

It was at that point I understood the message. After impact, her son didn't know that he was hit by the car; he was looking down at the accident and saying, *Oh my gosh, look what happened to Nicky.* His next statement was, *That's my motorcycle underneath the car. That's me who got killed and not Nicky.* As he looked at himself in spirit, he was wearing the exact same jacket as he had when he was alive. When you exit the body, there is no initial physical change in appearance.

The mother said that she hoped he had not felt the impact, nor suffered. The fact that he was looking at his own dead body, thinking it was his cousin, tells us that he did not feel any pain at all. He was unaware that he had left his physical body.

After a few more validating statements, I ended the reading. The audience applauded, and I had forgotten they were there. I was overwhelmed. I sat down and said to myself, "I want to do this."

James acknowledged that the reading I gave was good and then jokingly asked the parents why their son would choose to have me give the reading when he could have done it.

The mother stated, "The day after our son passed, he received word that he had been accepted to the Massachusetts State Police."

Later that afternoon, we did a meditation which focused on psychomerty. Rings, watches, and jewelry can retain energy imprints that can stay with an object for many years. To demonstrate that the energy can be read, we were asked to exchange something we were wearing with a stranger near us in the audience. A man sitting next to me introduced himself as Joe Higgins, as he was taking off his wristwatch. I took mine off, and we traded.

My watch was new; I had bought it the day before. Joe's watch looked like it had been worn a lot. The face was scratched, and the dial was yellowed. James started the angelic music and began the meditation.

Chuck Bergman

When it ended, I didn't have anything to report. Joe said that my watch was new, that I had bought it within the last day or so. He was right.

I looked at him and said, "This watch was worn by your dad. He just wore it when he went surf fishing." I clearly saw a man standing in the water with the sand and beach chair behind him. He had a large fishing rod and was casting into the ocean. As I was new to all of this, I was hesitant to give such a precise message, as I feared it would be wrong.

Funny you would say that," Joe smiled. "My dad was a doctor, and he owned three watches. One he would wear at work; the other when he went to dinner. He only wore this old one when he would go to the Cape and surf fish."

Joe and I became friends and would swap stories about readings. We later attended services at different Spiritualist Churches in New England. We kept an open mind and found humor in some of the presentations that we saw.

One phenomenon is called table tipping. For this, you need a small table. The sitters will place their fingertips on the table and summon a spirit that will rock or shake it. We were at my house in a room set up for meditation, and the ambiance was perfect. Joe and I sat for about three hours and tried to connect with our dearly departed loved ones. Unfortunately, the table never moved. Over the years, I have heard about such demonstrations being successful.

I was contacted by Adams Media to write a book as part of their Everything Series. I asked Joe if he was interested in co-writing the book with me. Joe had already written a book titled "Hello… Anyone Home?" He was ready and willing, and we started to work on "The Everything Guide to Evidence of the Afterlife." The book was published and offers scientific information along with personal stories of readings.

Joe and I keep in touch. We enjoy discussing our adventures, as we continue to become enlightened in spiritual matters

Two Diverse Worlds

Busted

I was summoned into the office of the Police Chief, Robert St. Pierre. Bob was a straight shooter. After he left college, he didn't know if he wanted to become a priest or a cop. As I entered his office, my stomach dropped as I saw James Van Praagh's website on the Chief's computer.

"Have a seat Charlie," he said. "We have to talk. How can I explain that I have an officer carrying a weapon who is known for hearing voices?" There was no easy escape for me. I responded that I had this ability as a child, and that I had been working very hard to develop it.

The Chief was concerned that court cases could be in jeopardy if defense attorneys learned that evidence could be coming from the spirit world. I reminded the Chief that we were, in fact, in Salem, MA, as I pointed to my police arm patch showing a witch riding on a broomstick. He was not amused.

An agreement was made that how I spent my personal time was my business, as long as the department was not involved. Word of an officer doing something like this traveled like wildfire. Many officers would come to my house for a session with the agreement that I kept it strictly confidential. Some mediums will use a stage name for this very reason. They want to keep it private, and apart, from their conventional jobs.

Past Life Regression

While on duty in the downtown area, two women approached me for directions .Detecting a British accent, I asked them where they were from. They told me London. The ladies stated that they had just published their first book together. They had come to Salem to celebrate.

I asked the name of the book. They told me and that it had to do with past lives. It seemed I couldn't escape this stuff.

I told them that I was a practicing medium, and that I was intrigued by the concept that we have all had past lives. They offered to give me a past life regression. I was most curious and receptive. I met with them in their hotel lobby early that evening. The session started similar to that of a meditation with the same calming, descriptive words to create a relaxed state of mind.

They then asked me to visualize myself standing on the peak of my house with my eyes closed. I was to walk to the edge without opening my eyes, step off, and float slowly down to the ground. I chuckled and stated that I was on the ground, and it didn't hurt. With my eyes still closed, I was to tilt my head downward, then open my eyes, and report what I was seeing. I started laughing out loud. I was clearly wearing Pilgrim shoes with buckles on them. They asked me what my name was. Without hesitation, I stated, "Mike Sullivan from New Haven, CT."

I knew that I owned a very small shop with another male. I could see myself arranging food and products very neatly on the shelves. In my present life, I have racks of food and household supplies in my basement resembling a small store; I am a neatnik. At the time, I wondered if my current basement store was a carryover from my past life. It was almost like a miniature Sam's Club.

Growing up in Florida, I often wondered why I was attracted to, and settled in, the New England States. Earlier in the book, I talked about Salem being so familiar to me as a stranger. More than likely, I had been there before.

Convincing Evidence

The Train

During one of my early readings, I met with a woman who had recently lost her son. The first image I saw was a Christmas tree with a model train going around the base of it. I wasn't sure how to interpret this image so decided not to report what I was seeing.

Next, I felt like I was sitting in a car at a train crossing watching the box cars pass in front of my face. I still didn't know what the message was. I, again, remained quiet.

In the next scene, I was standing on a bed of rocks between the two train rails. I shook my head and stated, "Your son is obsessed with trains." At that moment, I turned to my left and could feel the room shake, as I was looking directly at an oncoming locomotive. I relayed this to the woman.

She gasped and started to cry. She informed me that her son had taken his life by stepping in front of a moving train. I wish that I had talked about the train in a more pleasant fashion, such as circling the Christmas tree. This would have been gentler and kinder than the harsh manner in which I described it. It served to teach me to trust the images I am given. If I see it, I have to say it.

People often ask me do I filter. This means, do I sugar-coat information that I am receiving? Spirits want you to tell it like it is, and I have learned to trust what they give me. I've had to learn not to over-analyze the message I am getting but to simply put it out there. It is up to the receiver to interpret it. Words are the least effective means of communication. This may seem strange to us, but think about how many times words are misused or misconstrued. Spirits communicate more powerfully through feelings, emotions, and images. One of the benefits of learning spirit form of communication is that you can apply it to your daily experiences. Learn to trust the feelings and intuitions you receive.

All police officers depend upon their intuitive skills for survival. It is a necessary defense mechanism for them. When a case turned for the worse, I would reexamine what had happened to discover as many warning signs as possible. The next time a similar situation occurred, I was much more on guard. Most criminals are masters at disguising their real persona. Words can be manipulated. Gut feelings are almost always more reliable.

The Lottery

One afternoon, I was invited to a friend's house across the street for Margaritas. Little did I know that I was being set up for readings. My friend had his mother and her friends in because Chuck was going to be there. We ended up with a crowd of about twenty five. I was reluctant to do readings because I had had more than one Margarita before I realized why I was asked there.

My first two readings went very well, and I started to enjoy the environment. I moved on to Sally, a civilian worker at the police station. I told Sally that I was connecting with her mother and could tell that she had recently passed. "Sally, your mother is showing me a lottery machine, and it's spitting out money. She's pointing to you saying, *Thank you, thank you, thank you.*"

Sally said, "OMG." While visiting her mother at the nursing home, the room number kept haunting Sally. On her way home, she bought a lottery ticket with the numbers matching those above her mother's door. Sally won $10,000. Shortly thereafter, her mother passed away, and Sally used her winnings to send mom off in style. It was easy to understand why her mother was referring to the lottery ticket and saying "thank you."

Many more validations came in from her mom who ended by saying, *Play my room number tomorrow.* A week later I ran into Sally, and she was hugging me, all excited. The room number did, in fact, win the following day, but Sally had forgotten to play. Knowing what I know now, I should have placed my paycheck on that number. Every week, I ask my mom for the winning numbers-- but no dice.

9/II

In the fall of 2001, a lady came to me for an in-house reading in Salem, MA. When people book a reading with me, I prefer not to have any prior knowledge of their situation. After the usual greetings and explanation of how a reading works, I recall seeing a commercial plane on the ground. Through one of the windows, I could see a male waving at me and holding a cell phone up to the window. This rather innocent start to the reading played out to be very powerful.

I asked the lady if she could relate to this scene. She gave a simple, "Yes."

Next, I heard him say the words, *I wanted to say goodbye.* I was sitting in a seat on the aircraft and could feel the plane vibrating, shaking, and banking to the left. As I looked out the window, the plane was very low to the ground. I could see buildings and a river curving to the left. I saw myself, tray down in front of me, typing everything that was happening onto my laptop. I asked, "Did he own a laptop?"

She replied, "Yes, he did have a lap top, and if he bought a pack of gum, he recorded it there."

I was feeling what he had experienced at the time. He was certain that the plane was being hijacked, but his expectation was that it would land and the passengers would be held hostage. I saw him typing onto his laptop descriptions and actions of the hijackers.

It was then that I saw the floor of the plane opening up and all of the passengers' belongings falling down to the sidewalk below. I tilted my head upward and felt a calm peacefulness, as the other passengers and I were floating upward while still in our seats. I didn't hear any noise or feel any pain at the time of impact. I was puzzled as to what was happening as we ascended upwards.

Next, it felt like we were in a large, open room. Her husband told me that there were three wonderful beings assigned to each of the passengers. He said, *They knew we were coming.* He told me that those present were from the medical and counseling fields. I have since learned that, in the spirit world, angels typically work in groups of three.

I was confused when the image I was given was abruptly changed. I saw the husband stretched out in a recliner giving me two thumbs up and looking at a very large-screen TV. It seemed obvious to me that my glimpse into the other world was being censored. It was as if the subject was being changed or blocked.

The woman began to tell me the story. The reason for her husband showing the cell phone through the window as he waved was very symbolic of the morning of 9/11 when he boarded United Flight 175 from Boston to LA. He was trying to call his wife repeatedly to say "goodbye" because there was a real possibility that he would never see her again. It was obvious to him that they were being hijacked. This woman further told me that she was leaving her home that morning when the phone began ringing. She elected not to answer it at the time, but to let it go to voice mail, as she walked out the door. The caller was, in fact, her husband saying that he knew they were in trouble and that this could be his last chance to speak with his wife. Authorities did confiscate the voice mail messages for background sound analyses.

I had to ask why her husband would switch from such an angelic scene of being in the company of angels to a scene of him in a recliner watching a big-screen TV. This put a smile on her face as she explained that two days earlier, she had purchased a very large television. It was bundled with a free recliner as a bonus. It was scheduled to be delivered later in the week, and she wanted to ask her husband, in spirit, if she had done the right thing in making this purchase.

His two-thumbs-up jester, and smile on his face, made it very easy for me to tell her, "yes," he was happy with her decision.

The seemingly insignificant issue of the TV and recliner served to validate that her husband was around her in spirit at the time she bought them. He brought up the purchase and commented on his approval of it. He knew that was what she had planned to ask me during the session. He further knew that she wanted to know if he had suffered during the crash. That is why he so graphically allowed me to experience his final moments. Mere words would not have been as effective; I simply had to feel his ordeal in order to comfort his wife.

Later the same month, I attended a church service at the Swampscott Church of Spiritualism. The guest speaker was a medium from England. During the service, she selected people and gave messages from the other side. It wasn't until she was leaving the stage that she stopped, turned and pointed to me, and said, "Young man, I don't know what you do for work, but you have a lot of firemen in spirit standing around you. I think this has to do with 9/11." It was appropriate for me to acknowledge that I understood the message and to thank her.

Spirit World is Timeless

Spirit communication can include future information. A person may not understand or recognize a message from the medium at the time of reading. Often, that message will make perfect sense within a day or two. This is evidence that the medium is not simply reading the person's mind or picking up on their energy. Some spirit readings will offer information that will happen even as long as one year later.

This brings to mind a phone session with a mother who had lost her two sons in a house fire. Her routine was to have her next door neighbor look after her sons for one hour each afternoon until she got home from work. Unfortunately, the neighbor was not able to sit with the boys one particular day, so arrangements had to be made for them to stay at home alone for the one hour.

Their afternoon alone resulted in a tragic fire which claimed their lives. The mom wanted the reading to assure her that the boys were okay. She also carried enormous guilt for leaving them alone.

With much excitement, both boys came through clearly during the reading. The older boy wanted to say hello to Mike and described him as blonde and overweight. Their mother stated that Mike was the neighbor who typically watched the boys. It was apparent that the boys were quite fond of him.

I heard the name *Sally Jessy Raphael* and asked if the name had any significance. There was none. I knew I had clearly seen the face of Sally with her blonde hair and red glasses. While mom knew who Sally was, she saw no connection to her or her boys. I decided to move on. By the end of the reading, the name "Sally" was the one part that did not have any meaning.

The following day, I received an email from the mother expressing her gratitude for the reading. She told me that after our session, she went over to see Mike to let him know that her sons had specifically said hello to him by name. He responded by letting her know that he was going through his video tapes and came across one containing her two boys playing in his living room. He debated letting her know about the tape; he wasn't sure that she was ready to see it. The mom wanted to see it, but wanted Mike to watch it with her .That evening, they viewed the tape, and on it Mike's wife came out of the bedroom wearing a blonde wig and the red glasses. She was mocking Sally Jessy Raphael.

I continued to learn and grow with my psychic abilities. I used every opportunity I could to develop them while still maintaining my position on the Salem Police Department.

It was now time for a new chapter in my life. Retirement from the department was approaching, and I knew that this would give me more time to do what I loved the most. I had long wanted to return to my home State of Florida. I bought a house in Middleburg, just south of Jacksonville, my birthplace. I had brothers and sisters living in the area.

My first observation in the south was that most people did not have a clue as to who James Van Praagh, John Edwards or Sylvia Browne were. I could tell I had my work cut out for me.

In Florida, I started giving workshops and progressed to doing live radio shows. I went on to larger events such as speaking at the Florida Times Union Center in Jacksonville. I also did events in Boston, Philadelphia, Miami, and Amelia Island. I began working on high-profile police cases which opened new doors for me, especially with my police background.

Protective Mom

Lesley scheduled a phone reading with me a few months after her mother had passed away. The session was going well with the usual random validations. Around midpoint, I said, "Mom is telling me that your marriage is on the rocks. Is it true?"

"Things could be better."

"I don't know why, but I have to ask, are you talking to me on a cordless phone?"

"Yes."

"This may sound strange but mom wants you to stay on the line and walk into the master bedroom."

"I don't understand this at all."

"I don't either; I've never had a request like this before. She wants you to stand next to your husband's side of the bed."

"Chuck, this is getting a little strange."

"We have to trust that there must be a reason for the request. Mom is telling me that she wants you to look between the two mattresses."

"What?"

"Please, just take a look. Wait a minute, she is showing me a portable police scanner."

Lesley then looked under the mattress, where she found the scanner. "Is this a joke? How did you know that it was there?"

"I don't understand it either. Turn the radio on and see if you can hear my voice."

"Yes, I do hear you; why is mom doing this?"

"She's telling me that your husband is having an affair, and he has been monitoring your phone calls so that he will know whether or not you are on to him."

"That makes total sense now. When I talk to my friends on the phone, he will disappear to the bedroom and usually return when I get off the phone. He seemed to know my plans without me telling him. What should I do now?"

"For now, knowledge is power. Turn the radio off and put it back under the mattress."

Several months later, Lesley contacted me and informed me that her husband was, in fact, having an affair. She was able to track him using online credit card information. We are being watched in more ways than we know!

Coma

A friend of mine was curious about the possibility of communicating with a person in a coma. His friend, Denise, had been in a coma for five years as a result of a car accident. I had no idea if coherent messages could come out of a comatose state.

Denise's mother went with me and my friend to visit her at the nursing home. Denise displayed rapid, back-and-forth eye movement until someone spoke to her. Her eyes would stop, as if she were listening. Except for the eyes, she exhibited no other body movement. I sat next to her bed, held her hand, and mentally told her that I was there to try to communicate with her.

After about thirty minutes, I saw a frosted glass of water with ice cubes. The image was vivid, and I was certain that it was coming from Denise. I leaned near to her and said, "Would you like a glass of water?"

Denise's mother commented, "Some psychic you are. She has a feeding tube and can have nothing by mouth."

Next, Denise's two sisters entered the room. I asked, "Which one of you is Angel?" One of the girls acknowledged the name. I then said to Angel, "Your daughter looks just like Denise."

Angel replied, "Funny you would say that. We were looking at pictures this past weekend, and everyone commented on how much my daughter looks like my sister, Denise."

I heard Denise say to me, "Angel has a son, and his birthday is the same as yours, February 19." My birthday is, in fact, February 19. Angel confirmed this message. Angel and her sister completely changed the subject and discussed where to go for lunch.

While I was extremely excited about what had just happened, Denise's family chose to disregard the importance of the messages I had given to them. I had gone into the room with no information or background on any of the family members. I also felt that because of the feeding tube, Denise's mouth would be dry, and a cool glass of water would be what she must surely want. The statement about Angel's daughter would indicate that Denise, while in a comatose state, was able to travel outside her body. How else would Denise have known about the family looking at pictures in the album? And, how would Denise have known that my birth date was the same as Angel's son? Stay tuned!

Two Mothers' Stories

Yorhany

The following story was written and submitted for this book by Yorhany's mother, Barbie Pazos from Miami, FL.

Anyone who has faced the loss of a loved one, especially the loss of a child, can tell you that the only thing harder is to retell the story. It was with extreme difficulty that I sat down and put these words to paper. But if I am here at all, somewhat sane, coherent, and able to face the day, I owe it to Chuck Bergman. While Chuck and I met under the most difficult of circumstances, I have come to know him and see him for a gifted and talented individual. It is because of how much he has helped me that I can sit and share my story with others.

On a warm South Florida evening in mid June 2007, my life was forever changed. My only daughter and child, Yorhany Santi, was involved in a fatal car accident. Nothing could have prepared me for the next 12 hours, as I watched helplessly as the life drained from her body. I felt as if I were in a nightmare from which I desperately wanted to wake. That night I prayed and prayed to God not to take her, but my prayers went unanswered. I would have given anything and everything to have changed the circumstances leading up to that moment. Never had I so desperately wanted to turn back the clock, just to make a few simple decisions differently.

That day began like most other days. Yorhany was attending summer school to make up for a math class she had not done well in during the regular school year. She was going into 10th grade. I dropped her off at her school at 7:20 a.m. Ever since she was a child, we had a little game of who would get the goodbye kiss in first. That morning she was the one to get it in. We laughed, and I told her, "I love you; take care of you 'cause you're taking care of me."

And she smiled and said, "I love you mom."

Most mothers and daughters have issues in their relationships. I considered our relationship to be above the ordinary. She was my entire life, having separated and divorced from her father when she was very young; it had been just me and her facing the world. We shared many moments together filled with happiness and laughter. Financially, it wasn't always easy, but I tried to give her everything she wanted. Her happiness gave me mine. They say we live out our second childhood when we have children. I completely agree. I admit to being overly protective of her, but what parent wouldn't be. The world is not a pretty place, and I wanted no ugliness to touch my daughter. Don't get me wrong, we had disagreements, especially as she reached puberty. But the months leading up to the accident were some of the happiest times we shared together.

It was that summer that my daughter met her first official boyfriend. I wasn't all that crazy about it. It meant that my baby was growing up. I met with a lot of resistance, coming from a close knit Cuban family; both my mother and sister did not approve so much of this boy. Their main complaint was that he was a couple of years older than her, and already drove. But I saw that he genuinely cared for my daughter, and I trusted her judgment that he was the person who made her happy and that he would, above all, keep her safe. When she called and asked if he could pick her up from school that day, I said, "Yes" without hesitation. They were to grab a bite to eat, run a few errands and be home by 6p.m.

About 6 o'clock, we spoke, and I reminded her that she was running late. She assured me they were on their way. We texted back and forth for a short time. Then she stopped responding to my texts and phone calls. I knew immediately that something was wrong. I got into my car and went to look for them with only a general idea of where they might be. It was at that point I received a call from a police officer informing me that my daughter had been involved in a traffic accident and was being taken to the hospital. They wouldn't provide me with any details. By that time, my mind was racing with the fear and thoughts of what her condition might be. Was she in pain and calling out for me? The drive to the hospital seemed endless. The police officer who called me was kind enough to meet me at an intersection and escort me to the hospital. He stayed with me until I was allowed to see her. I should have known how serious the situation was, but I was in denial thinking everything would be alright as soon as I was allowed to see her.

On my way there, I called her father and her aunt because I needed to share my fears with someone, and I needed to hear from others that everything would be okay. None of us ever believed that she would not recover.

When I got to the hospital, I was told that she was in surgery. I still did not know what her injuries were. Shortly after the doctors met with me, they informed me that they had performed a CT scan and that the extent of her head trauma was too severe. Surgery at that time was not an option, and that the next 72 hours were critical. I sat and wondered how life could change so quickly from a day that started out like every other day. I felt as if someone had dropped a bucket of ice water on me. Yet strangely, and I can only express the feeling in this way, I felt warmth on my heart, letting me know that she was alright.

When we were finally allowed to see Yorhany, we thought everything would be okay. Even with the severity of her condition, outwardly she appeared fine. With the exception of a few facial cuts, she looked like she was in a deep sleep. In fact, the only trauma she really suffered was to her brain and a slight fracture to her left arm. She suffered no internal bleeding or damage to her spinal cord. We never stopped speaking to her, as we held on to the hope that if she made it through the next 72 hours, everything would be fine, and that she would recover.

The care she received was excellent. However, I can't say enough about the empathy and comfort the doctors, nurses, and hospital staff provided to her as a human being and to me and my family. Her nurses and her doctors were constantly at our side. Some of the nurses even wept. Most of my immediate family came that night to the ER. Every one of them was allowed to see Yorhany. Even her youngest cousin was allowed to touch her, hold her hands, and kiss her in what was to be their last goodbye.

As the night progressed, her condition deteriorated, and my despair grew. At some point after she suffered a crisis, the nurse spoke with us to let us know that we should consider a DNR (Do Not Resuscitate.) Without the DNR, in the event that her heart stopped, they would have to come in and try to resuscitate her, and the trauma on her person would be great. Given the extent of her head injuries, there would be little point in resuscitating her. For a while I could not bring myself to consider this option. I wanted to scream. I wanted run. I could not stand to be in my own skin watching what was unfolding before my eyes. This is the pain that every parent fears, and these are the decisions that every parent should never have to make.

As I mentioned before, during that night, I felt warmth on my heart reassuring me that she was alright. It was after her first serious setback that her aunt told Yorhany, through her tears, that everything would be okay, that she would look after me, and that she was free to begin her journey. She asked her mother, who had passed, to guide Yorhany and to watch over her.

The days that followed were equally horrific. Again, it felt as if I were in a cruel nightmare that never seemed to end. There were more decisions that needed to be made regarding funeral arrangements. No parent should ever have to make these types of decisions. As the realization of what had happened, and what I had lost, began to sink in, I became angrier at God for taking her. She was so young, barely having turned 15 years old. Why had this happened? Was there some lesson I had to learn, or had I done something to deserve this pain. All the while, I thought of the things she should have been able to experience, things that I would never share with her. Thinking about this just served to make me angrier.

The outpouring of sympathy was great and unexpected. I had always known that Yorhany had been popular and well-liked. In the months that followed, I was so very touched by the support of all those who had known her. Even those who had not were generous with their words and actions. I believed I was the only one lost in my grief, but I was wrong about that too. In the months and years that have followed, I must often console her friends, many of whom still post messages on her MySpace and on a Facebook page someone created for her. They told me what a caring and supportive friend she had been. How she had helped them through a particularly difficult moment or had simply been fun to be around. It was uplifting to hear from others what I already knew.

From the moment she was born, I knew how very special she was. Throughout her childhood, Yorhany constantly amazed me with her intelligence, sense of humor and maturity. At the age of 15, she looked 20. She was tall; her long light brown hair, honey colored eyes, and smile lit up any room she entered. Her voice was that of a little girl's, forever my little girl. She was boisterous and happy with a heart of gold. To her friends, she was a wise advice giver and a natural leader. She kept everyone in line, including me. She often befriended the new kid or the not-so-cool kid. She had dreams of becoming a special education teacher or of joining the Peace Corps. She was, and still is, my hero and my reason for living.

After the funeral, I could not, and to this day still have not been able to, return to the home we shared. Going back reminds me of all the things I lost. Her absence is all the more emphasized when I've gone back there. I did have to go and sort through her things. I came across an assignment that she had written when she was in the eighth grade. I've added her words to this story so that you, the reader, can also know my daughter through her own words. I've left her writing in its original form including the grammatical errors. The title of her assignment was "My Best Friend, My Angel" and it begins like this:

Friendship is a powerful force throughout our lives. Friendship must contain love, honest, and trust. What makes a good friend? A friend that you can have the memorable times with, that makes you feel happy and comfortable with yourself. Friends are like soundtracks of our lives. They make us feel better when we have a first broken hearts or when we need them the most. Friends are there to heal you, to pull you out of sadness, to brighten your day, and to clear your mind. Friends are there with open arms, to comfort you and to avoid you from trouble. To keep your secrets and entertain you when you want to play. Friends are there, smile or tears. Friends are there, happiness or fear. Friends are fun and friends are smart. Friends are people you have a special connection with and a special friendship that cannot be separated. There are special people that take the time to listen to all your problems and give you the best advice. Someone you can be yourself around with. Unfortunately, all friends get into fights but they always forgive each other. Good friends do not judge you by beauty or popularity, but by your personality.

My best friend she is indescribable. She doesn't judge me and she respects me. I have gained a bond with her that could never be separated. She encourages me to keep my dreams in sight, and shows me the obstacles of life and creates a smile on my face. She wipes all my tears away when I'm feeling sad and calms me down when I'm mad. She is my role model, sometimes I think she is perfect, even when I know she is human like me and you. Even when she does mistakes, she tries her hardest to fix her mistakes, that is what I love about her. This wonderful person is my mother. My mother has been here for me for the last thirteen years of my life, nonstop. She's always whispering in my ears "I love you". Even when I don't express myself and tell her how much I love her, she knows that I love her a lot. Not only being my mother, she is my best friend and my angel, I pray to God every day, and I'm thankful to God that I have a mother like her. Yorhany Santi

As you may guess, finding these words, although giving me a great sense of pride, also made me incredibly sad. When you are lost in grief, it's like you're empty. It's as if after all the tears have been shed, there is nothing left of your heart. The pain is so great that you feel a total void.

Misery loves company…when you go through something this devastating, you always come across others who have suffered similar loss. That is how I came to know Chuck. When I heard what Chuck had done for a mother who had also lost a child, I immediately set out to meet him. Many might say that people in such grief will hold on to the slightest bit of information given to them. I have never been a religious or even a spiritual person, never believed in an afterlife, never really gave much thought to it. I was lucky up until this point that I had all the people I loved alive and well in my life. I was one of those skeptics until my first meeting with Chuck. It's very hard to single out just one thing about that session. So many people expect to hear some revealing piece of information when, in actuality, the details come out in bits and pieces.

A little over a month after the accident, I made an appointment to meet Chuck. I really didn't know what to expect. I just needed to know about my daughter. I had so many questions. I remember as we drove up, thinking and asking her to provide me with a sign or an acknowledgment. I needed something that would let me know it was her and that Chuck was for real. What I really wanted was for her to acknowledge the "something" I had done special in her honor. I was hoping that it would come up in the conversation.

As we drove up to Chuck's home, I felt so many things all at once. I was lost in my grief and sadness and caught up with the excitement and hope that I would be able to communicate with her. I knew that I would never really hold her or touch her, but I needed her to know how much I loved and missed her and, above all, that I was not angry at her. I wanted and needed to know that she was okay. But more importantly, I needed to know that I had not lost her completely.

After getting slightly lost, we finally came upon Chuck's home in a lovely neighborhood outside of Jacksonville. It was certainly not what I thought it would be. It was a Sunday in late August. He met us at the door of his home and led us to a sunlit room overlooking an inviting back yard. Immediately I started to relax, as he began to make light conversation. The session was to be recorded, and I would later receive a copy of it. Before sitting down to write this, I tried to listen to the CD just to refresh my memory. But about half way through it I stopped, as I was crying so hard.

I now realize how important that first meeting was. Yes, I left there having connected with Yorhany. I knew that, regardless of our separation, the bond of love we shared was still very much intact. But I also realized that it was the first time I actually received a verbal confirmation from someone who had never met me or my daughter. Chuck was able to bridge and form a link between the existence in which we live with something more. The something we hope is out there, but which has never been confirmed, at least not to me until that first session.

Right off the bat, Chuck told me was that she was glad she had been the last one. I knew immediately that he was referring to that last kiss goodbye the morning of the accident. It had been the last conscious act between the two of us. As it turned out, it was the opening affirmation to what was to be a continuous flow of information between us.

He went on to describe events that occurred during the funeral. He told me that he wasn't sure, but there was something to do with a malfunction. I could not help but smile through the tears, as I later recounted to him how the lights had flickered during her Mass, and that the Mass had been conducted for a short period of time without electricity. I had no doubt that she had a hand in this. When this happened, I looked at other family members knowing that we all thought the same thing; this was something she would do just to lighten the mood.

Chuck also went on to describe that during the funeral, I was wearing, or holding, something of hers. That it was something that had the colors green and yellow. Throughout the entire funeral, during the viewing, at the Mass, and at the burial, I wore her school jacket which was green and yellow, her school colors. I wore it as a symbol of her embrace.

He spoke briefly about the circumstances surrounding her accident. He said that it happened rather quickly; it was noisy and that everything was spinning. He told me that there was a slight pain to the side of her face, and then everything went black. After that, she felt nothing, but she knew what had happened. She knew that she was no longer living. This was particularly difficult to hear, but he was accurate in his account.

The night of the accident, the detective working the scene described how it had occurred. The vehicle had gone airborne and had spun on two axes until it was stopped by two trees. My daughter received a blow to the right side of her face, causing severe blunt trauma and fracturing her jaw. She fell into a coma and never regained consciousness. When the doctors performed the CT scan, there was little or no brain activity. As the session went on, he told me details about the accident that no one could know or even guess. I could not bear the thought that she had suffered any pain or that her last conscious moments were filled with fear. Chuck provided me with the affirmation that she felt none of those things, and hearing that gave me much-needed peace of mind.

My daughter always wanted a tattoo, but I felt that she was too young to have one done. Shortly after her accident, I, along with other family members, decided to honor her desire by having one done. The tattoo I had done was in a location not easily visible. Still being somewhat skeptical about Chuck's abilities, and about whether or not the session was for real, I kept on asking my daughter in the days prior to the session to acknowledge the tattoo. This was the "special thing" I had done in her honor. This was the proof I was really looking for. During the session, Chuck told me that she kept on telling him to come over to me and raise my right pant leg. He thought for sure he would receive a slap to the face, so instead he simply asked me to raise it. When I did, he smiled and said he should have trusted her. And my daughter, having the sense of humor that apparently she still has, told him, *Yes, you should have.*

One of the things I found striking during the reading was the hand movements Chuck made. As a child, my daughter made a particular hand gesture when she was excited. It was really funny to most of us because when she did it, you knew she was really excited about what she was saying or what was going on. As best as I can describe it, she would hold out both of her arms and move her hands rapidly at the wrist, almost like saying hello but with both hands at the same time at about waist level. Sometimes, if she were really excited, she would jump up and down and move her hands all at once. She did this throughout her entire life. During the session there were a couple of times when we noticed Chuck mimicking the same gesture. We mentioned it to him at the end of the meeting, and he really couldn't remember doing it. It may have seemed coincidental that he would do the same hand movements, but when conversing with him in regular conversation, he doesn't do that at all.

Chuck asked us, or rather he told us, that we had gone through her things and mentioned that someone had laid on her bed and hugged her pillow. My very good friend, whom I refer to as her aunt throughout this piece, and who has been with me throughout this horrible ordeal, had gone into her room shortly after the accident, laid on Yorhany's unmade bed, and held her pillow. We both had to go through her belongings to put them away or donate them. I can't really say if this was another affirmation from Yorhany, or simply her not liking that we had invaded her privacy. He described her room and included the cherubs that decorated it. He also went on to mention that there was something about her room that she did not like, but that had been replaced with something bright. As it happens, one of the things she really didn't like was her bathroom. We had made a sorry attempt when we moved in to paint the walls a dark blue and add glow-in-the dark stars. She hated it. So, perhaps to occupy my time, I set out to improve all the things she wanted to change about her room that I had not been able to do prior to the accident. That included the remodeling of her bathroom. I had the bathroom vanity replaced and, with the help of her aunt, we painted the walls a bright orange. I realized as we took on these projects that most of what I was doing was really to keep my mind occupied, ignoring the reality that she wasn't going to be able to enjoy it. But when Chuck mentioned this, I was glad I had done it; she had noticed and she approved.

Her aunt and I made the trip up to Jacksonville to see Chuck together. Her relationship with my daughter had always been a special one. From birth, she was at my side and was one of the first people to hold her, feed her, and soothe her when she was inconsolable. The story of how those two bonded was a favorite one for my daughter's. As an infant, she played with Yorhany by raising her up in the air above her head. One day while playing with her, Yorhany spit up formula. The spit landed right in her aunt's mouth, and she had no choice but to swallow it. Their bond was sealed in spit. Gross, but she loved that story. Gloria and I have been friends for many years. She and I, both single mothers, often supported and consoled each other in difficult times. Yorhany spent many days in her company and in the company of her children whom she proudly claimed as her cousins. During the reading, many affirmations were directed to her such as her description as the "groomer"--someone who took care of others. She happens to own a Maltese Poodle mix that often required grooming. But Yorhany's description of her was more accurate as related to her being a caregiver. She was just that during my daughter's life and also in dealing with the details of her death. Therefore, it was not strange that Yorhany would describe her in this way. Her boys were also an important part of Yorhany's life. It was Gloria's eldest son who often picked her up at school that summer. Her relationship with the youngest can be described as siblings constantly bickering and teasing each other. It was no surprise that during the reading she snitched on him for smoking behind his mother's back.

One of the things that Chuck spoke of was where Yorhany was buried. He said that she was in one spot, but that he felt that it was just temporary. She would be moved elsewhere. This was a little-known fact that he brought to light. Yorhany was interred in a temporary location. The building that would house her permanently was under construction. We did move her several months later.

In a subsequent reading, Chuck mentioned her displeasure at the length of time that I spent at the cemetery by her crypt. He told me that to be close to her, I did not have to be there, that she was everywhere. I had a special picture of her framed on the stone of her crypt. She also made sure to let me know that she didn't like my obsession with kissing that picture all the time.

I left Chuck's home physically and emotionally drained, but more at peace than I had felt since the hours prior to the accident. After I received the CD of the session, I often listened to it on a daily basis. My connection to Yorhany was solidified by the contents of that CD. I admit, having that connection is what kept me from a total breakdown. I have been back to see Chuck a number of times, and each time I am not disappointed. I have no doubt that he is gifted and sincere. What he has given me, no church, priest or counselor has been able to do.

While I have learned to manage my grief, I know that it will never go away. My anger at losing her at such a young age has not disappeared but has mellowed with time. I recently began taking a yoga class in hopes of learning to meditate and calm my mind. My daughter used to say that I had adult ADD. I have no doubt that she was correct in her diagnosis. I have found that physical exertion helps me sleep at night better than any medication. Often, I walk at a park, and recently a group of young ponytailed girls came across my path. All the tears and sadness swelled up inside me and spilled out again. I miss her terribly, as I anxiously wait being reunited with her. Two things have kept me from seeking that path: knowing that she is still very much at my side and not wanting to disappoint her. As young as she was, she was a "get 'er done" type of person. She believed in keeping to her word and fulfilling her commitments. Taking that short cut would not honor her memory. I lived for my daughter, and as much as it pains me, I live for her still.

For me, grief is like being tunnel-visioned; you can't see anything along the peripheral edge. The affirmations we receive from our loved ones are like side bars in a court room, not really part of the official record but important to the case. Chuck taught me to pay more attention to those side bars. They let you know that you're not alone. For my family and me, the number 19 has great significance. It is the date of my birth as well as Yorhany's. It was also the exit number off of the highway where the accident occurred. It comes up a lot on a daily basis, whether it appears backwards, forwards, or in between. It just so happens that Chuck and I share that number, too, for his birthday and mine are the same. I wish that the circumstances of our meeting had been anything but different, but reaching out to him was the best thing that came out of that evening on that summer night in 2007.

Chuck gave voice to the affirmations given by my daughter, and that voice let me know that she is well. He confirmed for me that the love between my daughter and me is stronger than the passing from the physical world to the metaphysical world. Love, it seems, does conquer all. Most importantly, it continues long after the separation of our soul from the physical body. I believe now that life does continue, and that those we love never really leave us. Only our form changes; our energies remain to take on new structure.

I miss my daughter every moment of every day, but it soothes me to know that she is still right here with me. I know that one day, when my time on this Earth is through, I will see her again. There are no words that I can offer Chuck that would express the deep gratitude and peace he has brought to my life except to simply say, "Thank you Chuck."

Gloria Shepherd Story

I met with a family at a rooming house in Jacksonville where their son, Jason, had died. They had good reason to disagree with an autopsy report that cited toxicity overdose from Methadone as the cause of death. They were looking for answers about his demise.

I entered the room which was a typical efficiency. Family members were obviously in pain; having to return to their son's last home added even more hurt. The following are exact excerpts from the audio recording.

"I have a strong feeling that something is amiss here. I'm sensing something odd about the overhead light and the television set. Why aren't they on? Can you tell me anything about that?"

Gloria, the mother, answered and said, "When my son enters the room, the light goes on, and the TV goes on, and they never go off until he leaves. When he was found, both the light and TV in this room had been turned off. I knew because of that, something was not right."

"I'm a feeling of being totally disoriented. This is on the day that he passed, or possibly the day before. Does this make sense to you?"

"We think at the time it happened, there was a lot of confusion."

"Yes, he's not really sure about what's going on, but I want to predate it a little, maybe a couple of hours before then. I feel like there's another person involved here. Are you aware of that?"

"Yes, there is."

"I've got to tell you, I don't like this guy. He's rather dirty, and I feel he's dressed in dark colors, like maybe black or blue, as I see him. Was your son choked? Something going on in the throat, or choking?"

"If that happened, the medical examiner didn't find it."

"If he's injured in another way, could there be something going down the throat that would cause a choking feeling? I'm definitely feeling something in my throat. I feel like he's doing it to me. It's something he's remembering toward the end."

"We just don't know."

"Has he touched you; have you felt his touch? I saw the hand coming in; it felt like a real human touch."

"Yes," said Gloria, "I felt his touch. We were just talking about it the other day."

"He's bragging and taking credit for that, just so you know."

"That sounds like his personality."

"I'm trying to get him to tell me what happened, but he'll jump around. He still wants to prove it is him. People heard him, didn't they; they heard him yell? Either they didn't report it or didn't come to help? This was not a quiet event. Does that make sense?"

"He had a big fight here a few days earlier."

"I can take that, especially if he's trying to show me that it didn't happen in this room. The vocal part was like being out on the other side of the parking lot. I'm seeing street lamps, or I can see the busy street."

"I know that it was loud; he had gotten into a fight with Brian."

"I think you're right, Gloria. That would be the yelling that I heard. I feel that no one called the police."

"That was the Brian who worked with Jason. Brian always wears black."

"I'm getting a military connection with Jason, like the Navy?"

"He was going to join the Navy."

"He may still just be validating that it is him coming through. I'm clearly seeing a knife."

"His hands were swollen up the week before his passing because he got into a fight."

"Gloria, Jason is taking responsibility for his own passing."

"Yes, I think so."

"They didn't want it to happen in here. Someone wanted to lure him outside. I have a feeling they wanted to take him away from this area."

Gloria told me, "The door next door was kicked in, and I think that when Jason opened his door, they came into this room. The room next door was empty."

"I've got some squirming going on, on the bed. His death wasn't instant. It wasn't right away."

"That's what we think. We just want to know."

"I'm feeling something in the back of the throat on Jason. He seems to be throwing up."

"We know that."

"I'm getting that the perpetrator washed up in the room. Was there any evidence of that?"

"No, not to our knowledge."

"I'm getting these images, almost like when you're having daydreams. My focus is on the sink, someone washing their hands. This is after Jason has passed. Whatever they used, they're taking the evidence with them."

"The actual cause of death, according to the coroner was Methadone toxicity. They couldn't find it anywhere else but in the blood serum, three times the lethal dose, nothing in his stomach contents to suggest that he ingested anything except the 55 milligrams that was given to him that morning. It's the dosage he's been taking for a year and a half. They're saying his system just went crazy, and it took his life. It doesn't make sense to any of us. He was on Methadone to wean him off the drug use. He had, over time, cut the dosage down to the minimum amount, 55 milligrams, which should not have affected him as severely as the authorities are blaming."

"Was the air-conditioner off? Was it steamy or hot in the room?"

"The air-conditioner was on. It was freezing in here."

"Could he have been poisoned? He's showing me capsules, which could be symbolic of poison."

Gloria said, "I will tell you this, I was so convinced that the homicide detective just wanted to clear this case that I wrote to the Attorney General. I wanted somebody to get on the detective's ass. I got a call from the Sherriff. He told me that this detective did his job, that he himself went back to the medical examiner to check the contents of the stomach. They found nothing. Nothing had been ingested. No one could have given him anything that they didn't know about. He said there was no Methadone, or anything, in the contents of his stomach which is another whole question."

"I'm seeing two distinct capsules. Jason is saying he did not take an overdose."

"When they found him, he still had two pills left."

"Can you relate to a truck driver?"

"He was seen approaching a truck in the parking lot the day he passed. The property manager said he saw him carry a Styrofoam take-out container into the room. The autopsy showed he had recently ingested a full meal. I'd like to know who gave it to him. There was no Styrofoam container found left in the room. Apparently, someone purposely removed it."

"I'm getting symbols again. Whoever was in here was cleaning fingerprints. I see them intentionally cleaning up before leaving here. They knew he was dead."

"He didn't fight back at all?"

"Again, I've got him squirming; I can't understand what would make a person squirm like that -- like a convulsion, or severe cramping. He just said very clearly that he didn't make this happen; he didn't do it to himself."

"I know he didn't. We all know he didn't."

"Would this make sense to you because, as you say, the police are not cooperating properly or not questioning the people they should be. Jason is bullshit; he's kicking things, he's angry. He has a really angry side to him."

"Yes, Jason is wide open, whether he laughing or pissed, he's wide open."

"Okay, full-throttle. Who went to see the monkeys?"

"That's his nickname. We called him "Monkey" from the day he was born.

"He just showed me a monkey in a cage."

"Our family is a little off the chart. You'd be amazed what something might mean, so just throw it out. Feel free."

"Has anyone been to the beach recently?"

"I have, walking it."

"While you were at the beach, and I don't know why I'm getting this, could be that he just wants you to know that he was with you. I'm getting a negative with it. Like you didn't want to leave the beach that you just wanted to stay there, not go. I got a beach scene with him putting his arm around you."

"I knew that he was with me."

"There is what feels like a dispute going on, this is with another male. Like when you're really mad at someone, you hold them by the chin and shout at them. That's what I'm getting. I feel like this other person wanted to be mad at Jason for not doing or listening to something. Something about Jason trying to get his life in order, and he was almost there."

"That was me," said his father who was in the room." Several nights before he died, I grabbed him under the jaw, got in his face, and yelled at him that I was proud that he was finally getting his life together."

"I'm seeing a small boat; I'm seeing a boat, a bridge, and a ramp where you might put a boat in.

"He was acknowledging his father," said Gloria. "He has a small boat. He was giving him a validation."

"You were hard on him, mom, during his growing up, right? He's giving me a message that you treated him like you did the police."

"Yes, and I was harder on him as he got older."

"Is there a Las Vegas connection here? Has anyone been to Las Vegas?"

"I've been to Las Vegas with my friend, Joe. He's known as the one who likes to gamble."

"It's got to come down to what took him out. He's like a caged animal right now. He fuming; he's mad. He's referencing that he was just getting ready to talk to someone. Was the phone right by him when this happened?"

"Yes."

"Did he call someone?"

"He called his stepmother. That's the last call we are aware of."

"He's giving me the number eleven. It makes me feel like eleven minutes after that is when it happened, or maybe eleven o'clock."

"His stepmother said she missed a call from him at 10:27 am. He was found the next day."

"I have to ask why he's renting this place; is it temporary?"

"It was a tough love situation, and it worked. His fiancée told him "no more," I told him "no more." His father and brother told him the same thing. The party's over. After a few weeks, he was a different person. He had found God. He and his fiancée were getting back together, and they were looking for an apartment. He and his fiancée were happy. He was telling me that he was getting stronger, feeling better about things. Jason was a self-proclaimed atheist for fourteen years, until his son was born about five months ago. He began telling everybody that now he knew what people meant when they said they had been saved."

"There's something going into him, and I don't know what it is. It's like a liquid going down his throat. I'm seeing convulsions, the squirming. I think something had to be ingested to cause that. I have to ask-- no robbery or anything? Did they take his money?"

"No, nothing was taken."

"So what would be another person's motive?"

"We question that."

"You say he's been coming through to see other people since he's passed over. How's he treating them? Is he giving them any similar messages?"

"We've all seen him, but he won't leave his brother, Joey, alone. Joey is so exhausted and depressed over it. He has had very clear, explicit dreams. But Joey holds it in; he won't tell us. As a matter of fact, when Jason passed before anyone knew it, Joey woke up that morning and had a panic attack. He was upset and didn't know what was going on with his body. It was a feeling of terror and confusion, and then he got the call that they had just found Jason. He realized that it was Jason who was trying to get through to him. I know of one very specific dream that Joey had just recently. Jason said to Joey, *You're looking in the wrong place.* Joey was looking in someone's safe and found their gun, and Jason kept saying, *You're looking in the wrong place.*"

Gloria continued, "I had an incredibly explicit dream; I have no idea why. Jason was not in it. Neither one of the references made sense to me. But the dream hit me three times, bam, bam, bam. I fell asleep on the sofa in the middle of the afternoon. When my cell phone rang in my dream, I opened it, and there was the Days Inn logo, but on the logo with the sun was the word "Oleander." I didn't know what Oleander was. I had the same dream a second time. I asked Joe about Oleander. I wondered if it was a TV show. Joes didn't know either. I told him about my weird dream. We walked the dog, came back, had dinner, and I typed in "Oleander" on the Internet. I learned it was a poisonous plant. I had never heard of it before. The Days Inn logo was so detailed. There's a Days Inn on the beach not far from Jason's rooming house. I called my oldest son, Bobby, and told him about my dream and asked him to look up "Oleander."

"He called me back and said he thought Jason had told us everything we needed to know. He said he read about a guy on the Internet who had killed three of his wives before police discovered that he had poisoned them with the liquid of the Oleander plant. There is a very specific test to detect that poison."

I told her, "Dreams are their easiest and most common forms of communication."

"My dreams are always clear," said Gloria. "The day before Jason passed away, I was sitting at my desk working and felt a hand on my shoulder. I turned around, and nobody was there, and I immediately thought it was my father. I had not been speaking to him when he died, so I didn't know why he would come to me. Joe walked into the room that morning, and I told him I thought my father had just put his hand on my shoulder. I knew it was him. It was like a real touch. I realized the next morning that my father was telling me that my son had just passed away. He was comforting me. Do you know if Jason is with anybody?"

"They're all together, all of them. Would there be an older lady up there with bad knees, swollen knees? Maybe bad legs; I feel like it's more in the knee area?"

"Both of his grandmothers are still alive."

"I feel like it's an older lady with bad knees. She's a rather large lady; she's bent over."

"Does she have to be on the other side?"

"Is this description fitting someone with us here, now?"

"It sounds like my mom. We felt very guilty because we thought we had lost my mom in November; all our attention was focused on her. I almost didn't come here in January because I was worried about leaving her. But I'm glad I did, because that was the last time I got to see my son, and now my mom is working her way back to heath."

"That would be Jason's way of acknowledging her, wanting to say hello. That's the image that came in for me."

"She's on a walker and in psychical therapy for her knees. She's been very upset because she feels Jason hasn't come to her, but to everyone else."

"Let her know that he is acknowledging her."

"She will be very happy to hear about this."

"Was he cremated or buried?"

"He was cremated."

"I thought they're supposed to keep tissue samples."

"I do have the full autopsy report, and apparently you can petition to have the case reopened."

"Here's our problem now. Even if it was Oleander that was used, they did not test for it."

"They would have blood samples, I would assume," said Gloria.

"I still want to go back to the squirming part. It's almost like a snake, a feeling like trying to get away. I really don't feel like he was alone."

"The way they found him would not have been how he would have laid."

"Jason was extremely confused and baffled as to what was happening. I think someone came in here as a friend and did it to him without his knowledge."

"His girlfriend dropped him off at his room; he said he was starving and wanted to take a shower. She was to pick him up later that day. She kept calling and calling, and no one was answering. The next morning, she woke up late and called him at 8:15. She thought he must have caught the bus to go to the clinic. Then she got a call, and all she could understand was, "Jason, get to the hotel right away.""

"His father was called by the police and told that Jason had passed at the hotel."

"The hard part, Gloria, is where do you go from here?"

"I don't think Jason knew what happened to him; if he could have reached that phone, he would have. There was no sign of a struggle. One shoe was off, and one sock off; it doesn't make any sense. The air-conditioning was on freezing, and he was lying here with no shirt on. The reason why the maid stopped and became curious is because she didn't hear his TV. He kept his TV on all the time, and it was always really loud. He never turned off the TV whether he was in the room or not. The maid knocked on the door and alerted management of something strange. I'd also like to know where he got the food in his stomach. I wish we could have an image of who came to his room bearing food. Jason was found Tuesday morning with a freshly digested meal in his stomach. I think once Jason realized that he had ingested something toxic, there was nothing he could do; he went into convulsions."

"Could this other guy live at a Days Inn?"

"Possibly. It has something to do with the Days Inn. But in my dream, there was no color on the logo. It was grays--light grays, dark grays."

"Joe is Jason's brother? He won't share with you what he's getting from Jason?"

"Joe dreams of Jason; he has actually seen him by his dresser. Joe will see Jason at the end of the road where he used to always pick him up. Jason will just be standing there, smiling. Joe had a dream a few nights ago, and he said it was so horrible, he won't discuss it. He says Jason is saying *I'm still here*. I don't understand it all."

"That's typical, especially in a trauma situation. It's like he doesn't believe he's out of the body."

"We all feel his presence. His presence is very strong. When he's ready, he's ready; that's Jason. It's always on his terms. When he shows up, he shows up in a big way."

"Another thing they will do is go back to a point in time when they were the happiest, and they will present themselves as they were at that time. Sometimes, older people will show themselves as they were at the peak of their life, when they felt good, and everything was right."

"In my dream, he was 21 or 22; Jason was 29 when he passed. Today is the three-month anniversary."

"I think this is going to be a tough one. You're going to walk away knowing someone else did this, and that they're getting away with it."

"I know someone else did it. I know I can't bring Jason back, but he's in my heart and always will be."

Gloria and the family felt so strongly that Jason was misdiagnosed, that they hired an independent laboratory to perform extensive tests, using blood and tissue samples from her son. The laboratory reports concluded that the death was due to an extreme amount of poison being ingested by the victim. Police have reopened the case and classified it as a homicide.

Celebrity Readings

Bruce Lee

Following each broadcast of Psychic Search, the half-hour TV special in which I helped the Jacksonville Police solve a murder case, I receive numerous emails from people looking for help with either missing persons or unsolved crimes.

David Tadman, TV producer, writer and Bruce Lee historian, contacted me and said, "I watched your show, why don't you have a series? I've scanned the TV schedule looking for your name, and I don't see you anywhere!" I told him that doing a weekly show is something that I would be very much interested in.

David lives in California and has produced documentaries on Bruce Lee that have aired on The History Channel. He has also compiled many writings about Bruce that have been published. Bruce Lee was a Chinese-American, Hong Kong actor, a martial arts instructor, philosopher, film director, film producer, screenwriter, and founder of the Jeet Kune Do martial arts movement.

David proposed that he and Robert Lee, the only surviving brother of Bruce Lee, travel to Florida for the purpose of having a reading with me. The plan was to bring a camera crew and videotape the session to become a potential TV Pilot. Coordinating such an event can become costly and almost impossible to schedule. It made sense that I travel to Hollywood.

In the blink of an eye, I found myself sitting at the airport terminal with tickets in hand for Hollywood, California. The pressure was on! Several hours later, I was in a taxi cab on the California Freeway heading for my hotel room. David and I met over dinner and discussed the upcoming reading.

David invited me to meet his friend, Rubin, who owned an animation studio nearby. I was given a tour of the building, and I talked with several of the animators. I was shown the process they used in producing their latest movie, "Avatar."Rubin had arranged for me to be the guest speaker at their weekly discussion group at his studio. Their focus was typically on the paranormal.

For such short notice, there was a large group assembled. I explained that I was rather fatigued after my day of travel, and that I had to conserve energy for a videotaping the next day. The animators were able to edit down the thirty-minute version of "Psychic Search" to a ten-minute demonstration of my work. After the clip was shown, we conducted a question-and-answer session about my line of work.

One question I didn't expect, because it was supposed to be top secret, was "When are you going to do the Bruce Lee reading?" The kinds of questions were far more sophisticated than the ones I typically get from audiences in my area. One individual asked me if I would be able to pick up the presence of someone such as Michael Jackson, since he had just been in Michael's home. I told him that I was sure I would be able to connect with Michael in his own home and that I could leave "right now."

Even though I was not planning on giving any readings that night, a man named Jason asked me a question. I don't even remember what it was, as I simultaneously received a message for him. I said to him, "The last five Christmases have been very painful for you because a male figure has been missing. This Christmas will be even more painful because there will be two male figures missing." Jason stated that his father had walked out on them five years ago on Christmas day. This past summer, his brother passed away. So yes, there would be two males missing this year. Jason was choked up and started to cry, and I simply said, "I'm getting this information from William." Jason and several people around him, who had known his brother, expressed excitement that I had gotten the exact name.

To add humor and lightness to the moment, I suddenly extended my right hand into the air and began a circular motion and said, "Jason, William is doing this, and I can see a white cream on his fingertips.

He's telling me that you have to put this cream on down there," as I pointed to his privates.

This comment brought down the house. Jason's response was one of profanity which I will not repeat on this page. He tried to explain by saying, "The doctor just gave me a white cream this morning, but I do not have an STD. That's exactly the type of thing my brother would do -- embarrass me in front of a group." Hands went up from all over the room. Now they all wanted a reading. I did give a few more valid messages, but wanted to conserve my energy. After all, my mission was to do the Bruce Lee reading.

The next day, before our 6:00 p.m. Bruce Lee taping, David kindly showed me around tinsel town. Since I had never been to California before, I was intrigued. It was a good distraction for me, as it prevented me from being nervous about our upcoming event. We decided to do the taping in David's home, as he had turned it into a shrine for Bruce Lee. Sitting on a table was a pair of high-heeled boots worn by Bruce in many of his movies. A Buddha statue sat behind my chair. There were posters, family photos, and mementos everywhere I looked. Of course, there were the famous nun chucks. This was a setting far better than any studio could have replicated.

As the big hour approached, cameramen arrived and set up their equipment. Robert Lee and his wife, Jenny, arrived a short time later. Robert, the youngest of the five Lee children, had a commanding presence. He seemed excited and hopeful that I would be able to connect him with Bruce.

With cameras rolling, we did our formal introductions. I had no clue as to what my first question or statement would be. I thought to myself, "My first message should be something dramatic, something personal between Bruce and Robert. It should be something that neither the public nor I would have any way of knowing." I sat up nice and straight, and I said, "Bruce is doing this," as I simulated adjusting a necktie. "Bruce is showing me a cowboy string or a thin black tie."

Robert was startled and stated that about two days ago, he was going through his chest of drawers and found a thin black tie worn by Bruce in one of his movies. Robert had no idea how the tie had gotten mixed among his things after so many years and why he hadn't seen it sooner. He said that Bruce's personal belongings had long since been disposed of, and the tie was a true mystery.

I let Robert know that Bruce was with him yesterday as he drove his car and worried about something fragile in the back seat behind him.

Robert started laughing and said that he and his wife went shopping for his favorite ice cream yesterday, and rather than put it in the trunk, he put it in the backseat to keep it cooler. On the way home, his wife made him stop at several other places while the ice cream slowly melted. He thought it funny that I would mention this, as he had adamantly asked his wife to just go home.

I asked, "What about cartoon characters?" David told me that Bruce was always drawing stick figures on his scripts. David owned about 30 pages of those drawings.

"I'm hearing the word *fire*, like I'm on fire?"

David commented, "*I'm on fire* was Bruce's favorite saying."

I mentioned the word water, and David told us that Bruce's philosophy centered on water-- how it related to life. Many of Bruce's writings incorporated the influence of water.

"I just saw a large, furry dog and a hand rubbing the head. Bruce is excited about being with the dog; did he have a large dog?"

Robert told us that Bruce had a Great Dane named Bobo. David showed us a picture of Bruce ruffling the head of Bobo.

"I'm hearing that the money stopped?"

"Yes," Robert replied, "He was broke at one point; it was tough on him. He had people who mismanaged his money. It was not as glamorous as he thought it would be, but he still had to keep up his public image."

"Where are his remains? Where was he buried? Was there a conflict about another area wanting to claim rights?"

"Yes, people wanted my brother to be buried elsewhere."

"He wants you to know that he really doesn't care where his body is; it's his soul that matters. He just said that his spirit is everywhere."

Robert and David both reiterated, "He is an on-going legend."

I felt the energy shift, and I knew that I was now connecting with another deceased brother named Peter. "Peter wants to prove that it is him, and he's telling me that he was married to the most beautiful wife in the world."

Robert smiled, "Yes, she was gorgeous. In fact, she was Miss Hong Kong."

I said, "Peter should have been a teacher."

Robert replied, "He always wanted to be a teacher; that was his dream. He would have made a damn good one."

There were other good validations from Bruce, and Robert's mother and father came through with specific messages. After everyone left, and the cameramen were breaking down the cameras, I wasn't sure how successful the session had gone, so I asked to see the opening footage. Even though I know I had felt like my normal self during taping, on playback, I saw myself embodying a different posture. I seemed to have assumed Bruce's mannerisms.

The following comments were personally submitted by David Tadman:

"Chuck lays it on the line and holds no punches; he tells it like it is with a heart that is full of humanity.

When our paths crossed, I knew Chuck was a special person. To put it in simple terms, he cares about the ones who have passed on and about their families.

Another thing that amazed me about Chuck is that he has no ego or agenda, other than to help the ones who seek him out. He wants to bring closure to families and will not stop until there is justice for the fallen ones.

Chuck is also there like a therapist at your side to help you deal with, and to put into perspective, what has been done and what needs to be done. He is a teacher, mentor, and protector. Now, more than ever, we need Chuck Bergman."

David Tadman, Writer and Producer

RAY CHARLES

People ask me all the time if I am able to actually see the spirit I'm speaking with. Some give off a glow representing the size that they were when they were here. I can usually make out male or female. Some will show their chest and face area only, some just the face. There are some that have the ability to show themselves exactly like they were when they were here, in full body.

One afternoon I took a call from a woman named Lovie. She told me, "My sister is on the on the other line to make sure I don't give out any information."

"How can I help you?"

"We live in Jacksonville, and we want to have a reading with you in person."

"Do you have my address?"

"Yes."

"Is Thursday at noon good for you?"

"Yes"

"Okay, see you then."

I really didn't expect them to show up. I was wrong. The two sisters arrived on time and were ready to get the session underway. As they sat across from me, I turned my head to the right, and sitting on what should have been an empty sofa was a very prim and proper looking woman. She didn't come in with the two sisters, and she wasn't already in my house. She was as lifelike as the two women sitting in front of me. I decided to communicate with the older woman in the same manner that I talk to spirits.

"Hello, are you here to speak to the two ladies across from me?"

Yes, they are my daughters. I died last month from pneumonia.

"Ladies, are you here to connect with mom?"

"Yes."

"Did she die last month from pneumonia?"

"Yes!"

I didn't want to frighten the girls, but I was seeing their mother and talking to her like you would any living person. I continued for about twenty minutes when I heard the song "Georgia on My Mind."

"I'm hearing the song Georgia on My Mind. Do you understand?"

"Oh, yes!"

"I have to tell you, I'm hearing it being sung by Ray Charles with no accompaniment."

All of a sudden I heard Ray say, *Hey Chuck, tell them I'm here!*

I turned to look at the sofa again, and their mother was still there, and sitting to her left was Ray Charles wearing a white tee shirt and paisley boxer shorts. I seriously considered that it was time to check myself into a hospital.

"Why would your mother show up with Ray Charles?"

"Because Chuck, she is his mother."

"Say that again!"

"Yes, Ray is our brother."

Knowing that they would have to convince me of this, the sisters had brought the family photo album. I sat in my office looking at aged photographs of Ray Charles. In many were the two sisters and their mother, the exact same woman sitting on my sofa. I knew that there must be a reason why Ray showed himself in his underwear on my sofa. Up to this point, I had not mentioned to the girls his attire.

I started laughing and asked them, "Why would Ray be wearing a white tee shirt and paisley boxer shorts?" This made both sisters laugh. They told me that to protect mom's privacy, it was always kept a secret when Ray would visit her.

Lovie said, "One evening while Ray was walking around in his underwear, there was a knock at the door. Mom had Ray step into the closet while she answered it. It happened to be two police officers asking questions about vandalism in the neighborhood. It was hot in the closet, so Ray stepped out, much to the surprise of the officers." He exclaimed, "I can't stay in this damn closet another second." Lovie said that the underwear story was repeated at every family outing.

Both girls were quite pleased with the results of the reading. Lovie told me about how she decided to come to me for a reading. After Ray passed away, mom read a story about me in *The Florida Times Union* called "One of Us" written by Charlie Patton. She had wanted to have a reading with me as soon as she got well again. However, she passed before she could book that reading. One month after mom's passing, she came to Lovie in a dream and pointed to a folder on the desk. Her words were, *Read the story and trust this man.* The article in the folder was the *Times Union* piece, "One of Us" which featured me as a local psychic medium.

A Sense of Duty

TV Pilot Psychic Search

Because of my current work, I had a production company contact me with an interesting concept. They were producing a television pilot aimed at allowing people who claimed to have special abilities to prove those abilities. After submitting an audition video of myself, I was selected to appear in a show called "Psychic Search."

The premise of the show was to have me provide information on a six-year-old cold case in MacClenny, FL. A thirty-year-old male, Terry, had been missing for six years. I met with the family and two detectives from Jacksonville.

Because the TV show was somewhat challenging my claims of being able to contact the other side, I was extra careful not to jump to conclusions and label the missing person as "dead." I went to the first meeting armed with a piece of information that I did not share with the family, detectives, or producers of the show.

At 4:00 a.m. the morning that I was to meet with the group, I was awakened by an apparition standing next to my bed. I noticed that he was wearing a plaid, outdoor jacket. He was wet. He said, *I am going to help you.* He told me that his best friend had murdered him and had removed his body from a swampy area for dismemberment. As he turned to walk out of my room, I clearly observed mud on the back of his head and jacket.

I started the taping of the show by stating to the family that their son was not missing; he was deceased. The family expected to hear that conclusion.

There is a major difference in the way a missing person case is handled by police, in comparison to that of a murder case. It was necessary that I prove that I was in communication with their son by making statements that they would understand, but that I should have no way of knowing.

I addressed the victim's sister, Debbie. "Your brother is showing me small children around you, such as first or second graders." I asked if she was a teacher.

She said, "Yes, second grade."

I asked why she would use the word "halitosis" in front of such young children.

Debbie went on to explain how one of her students had just talked to a teacher across the hall and stated that he had very bad breath. Debbie informed her students that the term for bad breath was "halitosis." She tilted her head and asked me, "How would you know I said that?"

I let her know that her brother was with her in spirit and, still having a sense of humor, decided to prove his presence by repeating this unusual word.

During editing, that scene was cut by the producers, because they felt that no one would believe such an extraordinary validation. I felt that the expressions on the faces of the family, in response to that statement, were ones of total disbelief. Even the cameramen looked up from their view finders in astonishment.

I started describing the crime scene area, and I knew that we had crossed state line into Georgia. Detectives could tell by my description that it would be necessary to go to a swampy location where they had already searched. Upon arrival, we searched an area where I got very frustrated and kept saying, "We're in the wrong place, we're in the wrong place."

I saw a flash of the bedroom scene, which reminded me that Terry had been in water, and there was none around us. I pointed downhill and asked if there was a swamp in that wooded area, and the answer was, "Yes." When I saw the swamp, I knew we were in the right area. There was a mound of mud by the edge of the swamp, which coincided with the color and texture that I had seen on Terry's back.

I felt like I was reliving the murder. I described, accurately, the assailant to the detectives. I knew the body had been placed in a light blue pickup truck, which from the side appeared to have something that looked like a refrigerator, with the door removed, in the bed.

The detective showed me from his files a truck matching that description, with a dog kennel in the back, which had the same appearance of the one I had described. The truck had been used to transport the body back to the assailant's home in Florida.

I knew from Terry that his body had been dismembered. He was showing me a fifty-gallon drum, converted into a burn barrel, located in the center of the suspect's back yard. There was a lot riding on a burn barrel being in the back yard or not.

We traveled back into Florida to visit the suspect's home. Within a few miles of our destination, I was in the vehicle with the film crew when I felt the strong presence of Terry. I insisted that the driver pull to the side of the road, which he did. I paced around and felt high energy. The detectives watched as I bent over at the waist and made the statement, "I feel like everything is coming out of my head."

They informed me that our suspect had been stopped by police at that very spot and that he had shot himself as they approached.

We continued to the house and were denied access to the premises. While the negotiations were going on, I took advantage of the distraction to walk to the side of the house which gave me a clear view of the backyard. There, I saw a rusted, fifty-five gallon burn barrel in the center of the yard.

For legal reasons, many suspicions by the detectives were confirmed by statements given by Terry through me. As this type of evidence was not necessarily provable in court, it would be difficult to take action against other persons potentially involved. However, it confirmed what the police had discovered in the first place and reinforced their theories after six long years of investigation. It further brought comfort and closure to Terry's family because the truth was brought to light as a result of the TV show.

At the end of the five-day shoot, detectives upgraded Terry's case from missing status to murder. With all the information compiled, the case was officially closed.

Missing Teenagers

The parents of six missing teenage girls, living in a small community in Texas, asked me to assist in the search for their daughters. Police had been working on the case for four weeks with no success. I agreed to help.

On the flight, one of the stewardesses approached me saying that she knew me as a medium and needed my help in the back of the plane. A male steward, named Donald, received word that his fiancé had just died in a car crash. We were minutes away from landing in Texas. I was escorted to the compartment at the rear of the plane. The curtain was drawn to give us a little privacy. Understandably, Donald was traumatized. He told me that he had never experienced a medium before.

"That's okay, I told him; I've never given a reading on a plane."

I have to admit that it was a little distracting to tune into the spirit world while the captain was announcing, "fasten your seatbelts."

"Donald, I have someone here, and he wants me to say *Italy.*"

Donald became extremely emotional and said, "We were going to honeymoon in Italy."

I gave several more validations which calmed him down. It was rewarding that as I was exiting the plane, the pilot shook my hand and said, "Thank you for helping Donald."

My friend, Kristine, met me at the terminal. She is the one who recommended me to the families, as I had done a reading for her in the past.

Within an hour, I was standing in front of the parents of the missing girls along with Fred and James, the two detectives involved.

The meeting was videotaped and lasted an hour and a half. My focus went immediately to one of the missing girls, Ali.

"She's on the other side," I told the group.

I heard, *The person responsible is named R......* Both detectives looked up from their note pads and looked at each other in total surprise. For privacy reasons, I have not given out the entire name, even though I got it exactly correct.

I asked the detectives, "Would she have known a R…..?

Fred said, "Yes; Ali worked with a R….., and he quit the job the same day that Ali went missing. We have interviewed him, but we don't have enough evidence to take any action."

Events of the last two hours were happening so fast in my mind, I became a bit befuddled, as I tried to describe a location that I was seeing.

I said, "When you look at Texas on a map, I want to talk about the state to the right of us." I was having a difficult time remembering which state that was. I wanted to keep my focus on Ali, not on geography. I asked if there was a highway which cut a straight line across the State of Texas.

Fred said, "Yes, that's I-10."

I was being shown the eastern side of Louisiana, about a six-hour drive from where we were located. I described an area right off the highway. I just knew that was the place where Ali was buried. I asked, "Does this make sense to you?"

"Yes; that's the area where R…..'s parents live. He visits them every weekend."

"They're showing me an outdoor drive-in theatre under demolition."

Before we set out for Louisiana, the detectives had a couple of locations near Ali's home that they wanted to visit to see if I could pick up any vibes. The first place we went to, I did feel a slight connection with Ali. However, I did not feel that this area had anything to do with her disappearance. We started to make our way to the highway when a radio message from an unmarked cruiser, just ahead of us, came over the speaker.

"Tell Chuck to look to the right."

Coming up in front of us was an outdoor drive-in movie, and a crane was taking down the screen. I knew that we were on the right path and that we were getting accurate information. We were intercepted by a female detective who insisted that the body was in this area. She claimed that at three o'clock that morning, she stood at the end of her driveway and was able to talk to Ali in spirit. We ended up following this detective to several locations, all of which produced no evidence. I felt that this time spent was for naught, as we should be focusing on Louisiana.

Around lunch time the same day, the decision was made to make the six-hour drive across the state line. Plans were set into action because of jurisdictional issues between law enforcement agencies. Once in the eastern part of Louisiana, I recognized several landmarks that I had described in my earlier reading the day before. However, the one sign that I was specifically looking to find eluded us. I know that, during my reading, I had seen a hilly field with a sign on it that read, "Lease." To the right of that sign should be a driveway with white sand. I felt strongly that this is where the body would be found.

As luck would have it, heavy traffic had taken us longer than we expected, and we had no plans to spend the night. You can imagine my frustration that we were so close, yet had to abandon our search. The field, the sign, the driveway were so imprinted on my brain, that I knew I would recognize them immediately. As we were returning back to Texas, the detectives checked in with the Captain. He said, "We gave him twenty four hours, no body, cut him loose." Both detectives pleaded for twenty minutes that I had corroborated their theories, and we needed more time.

I later learned that the female detective, who claimed to have psychic abilities, had an "in" with the powers-to-be. She wanted to take over the case.

The following afternoon, Kristine and I went to lunch at the hamburger place where Ali and R….. had worked. As we sat down at a table in the center of the room, I pointed to a row of booths and said, "No, I want to sit over there." I didn't know why. We moved to a booth, and I was hoping to pick up energy from Ali. For some reason, I noticed that the sideboard to Kristine's left had laminated wood that was separating. I zeroed in on something white inside the peeling wood. I used a fork to pull the object out. It was a folded 8 ½ x 11 sheet of paper.

On the front of the paper was an intricate drawing of a woman in running clothes. I got chills right away, as I remembered seeing similar drawings while visiting Ali's bedroom with her parents. On the flip side was the sketch of a gravesite with a hand coming out of the dirt. Shown below that was a person's head with a semi-automatic 45-caliber pistol pointed at it. I definitely felt that this drawing was done by Ali. We later took the sketch to Ali's parents to see if they would recognize it as their daughter's. Both confirmed that it was absolutely her style. I recommended that they turn the drawing over to the detectives.

It was time for me to leave. One has to question what guided me to the restaurant, and why did I, and not someone else, find this hidden piece of paper. Was Ali's choice to draw such a graphic death scene, at only 16 years of age, a premonition or a clue?

As of a year later, the other missing girls have returned home. Ali remains a missing person case.

Missing Banker

I was finishing a phone reading with a woman who lived not far from me, in Jacksonville. The session lasted for over an hour, and I was feeling drained and ready to kick back and watch TV.

As an afterthought, the woman stated that her brother-in-law, from Michigan, had been missing for seven days. She wanted to know if I could get anything on him.

I explained that if he were on the other side and started giving me messages, she would have to be able to recognize or validate them. She didn't know enough about him, personally, to answer many questions. I suggested that some family member book a reading, and if he were on the other side, he would come through.

I continued with her, to see if she would recognize any messages I was getting.

"I see stacks of money, a vault, and I feel like I am inside a bank. Do you relate to any of this?"

"Yes, he's a bank president."

"Okay. I see very shallow water; I see him lying on his back, not completely submerged. He has a bullet in the back of his head. He was murdered."

She replied, "I don't know about any of that. I just know that he's been missing for seven days."

We ended the session. The following day, I mailed a CD copy of her reading. She sent the CD to her sister, the missing man's wife.

One week after that, I received an email stating that duck hunters had found the body in an area of shallow water. She further told me that the death had been ruled a suicide, based upon the fact that he still had money in his wallet and his cell phone with him. The wife had reason to believe that this was absolutely no suicide. After listening to my CD, she took it to authorities. This resulted in a second autopsy being ordered. Within minutes the pathologist located the bullet hole behind the head.

About six months later, I had a call from an attorney representing the wife of the deceased banker. I was asked to fly to Michigan to visit the crime scene with the wife to see if I could get further information.

I flew in to Michigan and met with the wife at her home in preparation for our trip the next day to the crime scene. That morning, we both had to scale a chain link fence to get to the water's edge where he had been found. The husband came through and let me know that there were two other people involved. He told me that his life had just turned around and everything was going in a positive direction.

It's my experience that a person responsible for taking his own life will always reference that it was the wrong thing to do. I was certain that he did not take his own life. I started giving messages involving their personal lives, which were confirmed by the wife. She commented that, at one point, my mannerisms and choice of words mirrored those of her husband. I then came up with a man's initials and felt that he had something to do with the case.

"Can you think of someone relevant who would have the initials RM?"

"No."

"I gave the first and last name and asked if he worked for the Federal Government?"

"Yes, my husband talked to him the night he went missing."

When the authorities questioned this man, who is older, he feigned a lack of memory.

Other pertinent details came out of the reading, but because of the on-going investigation, I cannot divulge certain information.

Just when I thought we were done with the reading, the wife's mother came through.

"Who is Virginia, I asked?"

"That's my mother."

"She's talking about the cream you put on your skin and saying, *It burns, it burns.*"

"I just had a face peel."

The mother continued with personal family validations and words of encouragement. The mother also verified that this was not a suicide.

Before leaving town, I attended a large meeting with investigators, attorneys and family members. All were hopeful that more messages or details would be forthcoming. None was.

Spirit can only give us so much information. I felt this man gave us all that he knew.

Finding the Body

A family contacted me from California. Their son had been missing for eight months. Police had given up searching. They suggested that the family contact a psychic. I was able to give them a reading that evening.

I immediately saw the bloody fingertips of a male. I could tell he was rock climber. His mother stated that her missing son was, in fact, an avid rock climber.

Early on, the son let me know that he had been having problems and that the "wedding was off." This was a fact that mother well knew about. After about twenty minutes of proof that I was talking to her son, he asked that mom take out a map of the area and place an "X" on her home.

I felt that this was a strange message, as I didn't know where I would be going next. I could see the numbers "020" which I recognized as being a compass heading of northeast. Next I saw a green Chevrolet pickup truck in poor condition.

The mother said that this totally described her son's truck. I felt like I was sitting in the front seat, holding onto the steering wheel, and looking at large rocks in front of me. It was like a movie camera panning down, and zooming in, on the instrument panel. The trip meter clearly read, "159." I told the family to draw a line from the "X" of their home "020" degrees, "159" miles away. "This location is where you will find his pickup truck, and you will find his body next to it" We closed out the reading and said our goodbyes.

This was the first time that I had strayed from giving traditional, verifiable readings. I felt that I had put myself out on a limb and wanted to throw my phone against the wall in frustration. I wondered, "What if their son returns home?" I would look like a fool. Truth be told, I would be happy for him and family if that were the case, but I would never offer to do that type of reading again.

Twenty four hours after my reading, I received a call from the mother. She had gone to the authorities in the jurisdiction of the area I had described. They sent a helicopter over the exact coordinates I had given. From the air, they spotted the green Chevy pickup truck. The terrain was rough and could only be reached by four-wheel ATVs. Investigators found his remains next to his truck.

Missing persons' cases present a special challenge. I know that if I misinterpret something, I risk changing the entire dynamics of the situation. I know that I must be precise and that all information is time-sensitive. Typically, investigators have to put many man hours into a case, and I have to be cautious about giving messages that would interfere with their due process. Facts that I might come up with could inadvertently give away privileged information.

Missing in Germany

As luck would have it, a short time later, I received a call from a family whose son went missing after attending a concert in Germany. The family was from Tennessee, and their son was attending college in Germany. He and his roommate were last seen inebriated in a large crowd. Later that night, the roommate returned home, but did not hear from his friend for three days.

A search was initiated, and the parents flew over to Germany to assist. I was referred to them for a reading. The father was very skeptical, but they were desperate. We agreed to hook up on Skype. I did my usual few minutes of validations. I had to break the bad news that their son was on the other side.

I saw a Raven and felt quite confused. I finally stated that I didn't understand the significance, but that I was seeing a Raven very clearly. The Raven was right in my face. The mother told me that she had just received a text message from a close friend in Sedona, AZ, who was a Native American. He was a Psychic but had failed to connect with her son. The text read, "I don't know what you're doing now, but I am being told that you are talking to the Raven, and the Raven never lies." I always related "The Raven" to Edgar Allen Poe. It gave me a new perspective and respect that many forces were joining together to bring closure to the family.

During the reading, I saw a river bank with large stones leading down to the water's edge. I could feel their son slipping into the water and his panic as he tried to scale up the rocks to safety. The father interjected that they had just searched such a location earlier in the day. He said that there was no way a body would go unnoticed, as it was shallow there with no current. A short time later, I concluded the reading with the same findings that their son was on the other side and drowned in that river. The father politely said, "Chuck, I pray that you are wrong." I said, "I hope so too, but I know that what I am getting is correct."

Three days later, I received an email stating that the body had been recovered on the river bank previously searched. Apparently, the current did move it. The family was grateful for my information, and I have heard from them several times since.

Gallery Readings

Cypress Club

After moving to Florida, the first public gallery reading session I did was at the Cypress Club in Orange Park. There were about one hundred people in attendance. I observed a young man having problems getting in the door, as seating was limited, and we had reached our maximum. He was pleading with the ticket taker to let him in. I made the decision to let him come in anyway; we would find room.

The show started normally and was going well. I singled out the young man, Eric, who had been adamant to get in and said, "You shouldn't be alive."

He started crying. I asked him to come up on stage. To make it more personal, we put our two chairs face to face.

"I have just picked up on a female friend who has recently died in a car accident. She is apologizing for how you learned about her death."

Eric began his story. "Both she and I had just moved to Florida from New York. She used my car to run an errand. I was supposed to have gone with her, but did not. For whatever reason, she became involved in a police pursuit, lost control of the vehicle, struck a tree and died. Police were unable to contact next of kin because my license plates were registered in New York. I worried all night because she had not returned. The next morning, I turned on the TV and saw pictures of my car wrapped around a tree. Police were requesting public information regarding this fatal accident."

"She's telling me that she made wrong choices and doesn't blame you. She realizes that she, alone, is responsible for her actions."

Eric came to the meeting in desperation because of his guilt about not being in the car with his girlfriend. He felt that he should have died, too. In fact, he let me know that he had been contemplating taking his own life.

I kept in touch with Eric for several days and saw a marked improvement with time. I often wondered what the outcome would have been if he had been refused admittance to the event.

Amelia Island

At another event in Amelia Island, FL, I stepped down from the stage and placed a chair in front a girl sitting in the front row.

"I'm being told that you need a reading, but you're very nervous, so I want to make it easy for you." I sat directly in front of her, held her hands, and told her to allow the rest of the audience to disappear. I've got a five-year-old female calling you mommy. Did you lose your daughter?"

She replied, "Yes."

"I'm hearing a "T" sound for her name; sounds like Teresa?"

"Her name is Teresa."

"You're worried that she's alone up there, but she's not. She's with another family member whose name also starts with the letter "T." Do you know who that might be?"

"No, I don't think so. But wait, I lost my sister, Tina; could that be the "T" name?"

"Tina, yeah, that's a "T." The audience laughed.

She started shaking and crying, and was very happy, which answered her own question. It was her sister watching her daughter.

Spirits will communicate their names in many different ways. Some will show me the face of a person to whom I can relate and, therefore, be able to state the actual name. Sometimes I will pick up only the middle of the name. Some never give their names during a reading but offer other meaningful information. It's a mistake to have preconceived ideas of the exact message you want to receive. Spirit will give you the content they want in the manner in which they wish to deliver it. Even if you are skeptical, it is important to keep an open mind.

Jacksonville Ramada Inn

I did a group reading at a Holiday Inn in Jacksonville for about twenty five people. A young man named Jose had called me two days earlier and asked about whether admission guaranteed getting a reading. He would have an eight-hour drive from Miami to Jacksonville and wanted some assurance that he might be selected. I explained that I can only give out messages that are given to me from the spirit world. I cannot predict, nor guarantee, who those messages are meant for. For some, hearing that our loved ones are around us is all they are looking for. There is great pleasure in hearing the messages and witnessing the peace and healing that they bring to the entire audience.

During the session I was drawn to a good looking, well-dressed young man in the front row. I had no idea what Jose, from Miami, looked like. I walked over to him and said, "I believe we talked on the phone, and you drove up from Miami? Did you find a friend to drive with you?"

He said, "No, I came alone."

I felt strongly that he had a real need to be here. "You're going through a hard time, aren't you? Your grandmother is coming through and saying that you have to make a change, or a move. Do you know what that means?"

"Yes," he said, with tears in his eyes.

I was distracted by a comment made by another person, when I suddenly turned back to the young man and said with surprise, "You almost died didn't you?"

With tears now flowing, he said, softly, "I tried to commit suicide the other day."

"Your grandmother is showing me that you were signing legal papers recently."

"Yes, yesterday I was arrested, and the papers had to do with me and my roommate."

"Grandmother is saying that you did the right thing. There will be changes for you, both in your work and where you live."

By revealing his secret that night, it seemed to give the young man a release, and he was able to later interact with other people in the room who had experienced similar pain.

During the three-hour session, I read twenty to twenty five people. Some received brief messages, while others were given detailed and lengthy information. In particular, was a lady who had lost her husband two years ago. I saw her husband fall onto something like a dock. I also saw a BP Oil sign and asked her if that was relevant.

She said, "Yes, he worked for BP." She said that he had a serious accident with them involving a fall that broke his leg and back. He was on heavy medications.

I told her that I felt that he was difficult to live with.

She said, "Yes."

I told her that he was saying something about an empty towel rack. She said that he was always upset with her about trivial things. One particular annoyance was that she never put the towels back on the rack. I strongly smelled diesel fuel and asked her about that. She said that her husband worked on diesel ship engines and always smelled of diesel fuel.

I had moved on to another person in the group when the previous woman's husband interrupted the reading. He was insistent to be heard again. I turned back to her and said with amusement, "Shrek?" I could clearly see the green, ugly face before me.

She said, "Yes, that was my nickname for him. No one else called him that.

"He is showing me a large doll with a human-like, porcelain face."

"I don't understand that."

I decided to let it go and move on to another person in the group. The next day I received an email from the lady stating that when she opened the door to one of her closets, there was a large doll with a porcelain face sitting in the corner. She remembered that when her husband first started working below decks on the tankers, he found and came home with the doll. It had been in the closet for years. The doll is now in her living room and serves as a reminder that her husband is with her always.

That same night, a father and daughter were in the audience, and I gave them messages from the wife/mother. "For some reason, she's talking about Thanksgiving, and I'm feeling negative about it."

With tears in his eyes, the husband said, "She died around Thanksgiving, and we no longer celebrate that holiday."

"She's showing me pictures with large letters being added to them. Does this mean anything to you?" The daughter said that she had been working on a collage of pictures of mom and had been putting large text descriptions onto them. This was mom's way of proving to her family that she is around and aware of what they are doing.

The coup de grace was when I pointed to the father and said, "You're slipping your daughter some money."

The daughter laughed and said, "I was hoping mom would come through and tell dad to please lend me some money."

Reading Techniques

How Would You Communicate?

Try putting yourself on the other side. Imagine that it is you in the spirit world trying to communicate with a loved one here on earth. What word or image would you use to convince someone that it is really you? It is not as easy as it might seem. As many things as you and a loved may have done or experienced together, they can be quite generic when trying to express them. It takes something unique and known only to the two of you to really drive the point home.

It takes a lot of energy for spirits to come through with messages, so they must try to keep them as short and concise as possible. It is also a challenge for the medium to understand and deliver the message. If the sitter does not seem to recognize the message as it is presented, it is a further test for the medium to try to interpret it. It is always a three-way communication.

Try this exercise with a friend or spouse. Ask each other to come up with one quick, short message that would clearly make the other understand who was speaking from the spirit world.

The following is a good example from one reading where a lady quickly identified my message of only a few short words. To make it even more challenging, this session took place in a group of about twenty people. I did not single out any individual, but said, "Why am I seeing an empty paper bag, like a little brown lunch bag?" When no one answered, suddenly the lady in the audience started laughing.

"Oh my gosh. That's my husband. This goes back over thirty years ago. When we were dating, he used to spend the night at my house and always brought a small paper bag with his toiletries in them. It was a big joke about him and his "little paper bag." Even his now-grown sons made fun of dad and that "brown paper bag." I told her, "He's laughing now." She definitely knew the message was for her alone.

In today's world, everyone uses plastic bags. He had to show me the small, paper one to be explicit. To have shown me toothbrush, shaving cream, etc. in it would have taken too much energy. Fortunately, the lady was paying attention, which is so important. You must stay acutely attuned to the messages; otherwise, you could miss something significant.

Three Way Communication

The outcome of a "successful" reading depends upon many factors. It is always a three-way communication among the medium, the spirit, and the sitter (the person receiving the reading.) If the sitter is expecting a specific word or phrase from the spirit, his or her focus will be distracted from the true message that may be coming in. Some mediums refer to this as "blocking" messages. The medium has a difficult time delivering messages to a sitter who exhibits a negative attitude.

As an example, I recently did a reading for a woman whose husband had passed several years ago. Their 30-year-old daughter was also present. I brought the husband through with many accurate validations, as often verified by the daughter. The mother seemed resistant to the messages and would cross her arms and continue to say, "No" to most of them. The daughter would correct her and remind her of certain instances. The mother was "blocking" important messages because she was stubbornly waiting for that "secret" phrase from her husband. I kept reminding her that it does not always work that way. Spirit has a free will; looking for a specific is really testing them. We know they remember things like names, dates, and social security numbers. What may seem important to us in this lifetime, they may consider trivial.

This particular reading was important to me, as the woman was a friend of my very good friend, and I didn't want to fail. With her attitude, I felt that I had done less than my best. However, I later learned that she told other friends that it was the best reading she had ever had, and she has had many.

There are more obvious forms of communication than the spoken word. Attitudes, body language, gestures and mannerisms express volumes. The medium is particularly sensitive to all of these. One-on-one, these signs are easily observable. During a phone reading, the medium must be intuitive and alert as to how the message is being received. The more positive feedback a sitter gives, the more encouraged the medium and spirit become. The analogy is a football game; the more the crowd cheers, the more it spurs the players on.

Spirits look for every opportunity to let us know that they are okay and that they are around us. Many people will have a first-time experience with a spirit shortly after the passing of a close family member or friend. The initial contact is usually unexpected. The most common occurrence is to recognize a familiar smell associated with the person who has passed. This can happen at a time when you are not even thinking of them. When this happens, the aroma is very real. Most people will inhale several times in disbelief. The feeling is that of euphoria and the knowing that the loved one has paid a visit.

Hours before I do a reading, it is common for me to visualize the person who made the appointment and to get a feel for who they may want to contact. This may seem like an impossible challenge, but it does happen. This is called precognitive recognition. If I ask for the spirits to come to me ahead of time, they usually do. I get a distinct feeing of heightened energy. It is like an affirmation planted in my brain, and I'm not sure how it got there. It is the "knowing" of a certainty. I have learned to recognize whether it is my own thought or a message from spirit. This gift has been finely tuned through hours of meditation and practical experience in dealing with so many people.

An example of this type of precognition happened to me recently. I was talking with a friend when I noticed that I had to return to my office to do a reading. He asked me, "Oh, who are you reading?" All I knew was that my next appointment was a phone reading for a woman in Ohio. I then said to my friend, "This woman wants to contact her father, and his name is Bill. He is a first-class petty officer." This information just came to me.

A short time later, I placed the call to the client. I immediately asked, "Are you hoping to contact our dad?"

"Yes," she said.

"Is his name Bill?"

"Yes."

"Was he a first-class petty officer?"

"Funny you would ask that. Dad died recently, and I typed out his obituary to email to my brother. He said that everything was correct except that I had forgotten to include that dad was a first-class petty officer."She told me she had to email her brother back to ask what that meant. It amused her that I would use that term or would even know that it related to her father.

Waste of Time

A woman made an eight-hour drive to visit my home for a reading. When she sat down, she tucked both feet under her and sat sideways, not facing me. She was chewing on a seven-inch straw. I wasn't sure if this was a sign of nervousness or disrespect. She started off by stating, "I'm not sure why I'm doing this."

This was not a good sign for me. I asked if there was anyone, in particular, that she wanted to contact.

She casually said, "Well my mom and dad have passed."

I felt the presence of a male energy, and he had the feeling of being family-connected."I'm hearing the words *homicide, police detective, and unsolved case.*" Do these have meaning to you?"

She said, "My dad died in a nursing home; I guess if you tried the food there, you could consider that murder."

This reading was not going well. I felt a little embarrassed and asked if she could recognize a woman coming through. I got very specific about her passing, hoping that this would be her mom. I described her as a heavy smoker, and I could see blackened lungs.

She countered, "She never smoked."

I continued, "Her name starts with the letter L?"

She abruptly said, "Nope."

I struggled for another ten minutes and finally terminated the session in frustration.

She turned to leave and asked, "Maybe you can contact my brother?" He was murdered two years ago, and they never found out who did it."

I threw up my hands and said, "Did you hear me say the words, *homicide, police detective, and unsolved case?*"

She replied, "I thought you were talking about my dad."

A lot goes into preparing myself for a reading. It sometimes takes hours, or even days. I visualize, literally, being with the spirit. I try to feel the love the spirit will have for the person wanting the session. Most importantly, I must block out any indicator that could give me preconceived information. In essence, this woman had "shut me down" during the reading, and it was impossible for me to readily reconnect with her brother.

Two hours later, this same woman called my house asking if she could return the next day. She said that on her way home, she remembered that her mother-in-law, Linda, passed away last month from lung cancer. I declined to do a second reading for her. She totally drained my energy and created a negative environment that I didn't want to repeat. Realistically, I expect one or two of these kinds of experiences a year.

Attention Dad

A male called to book an in-house appointment with me. It was the beginning of the week, and I showed an opening for the upcoming Wednesday afternoon. The caller informed me that he would be coming up from Miami, which is about an eight-hour drive. We agreed upon a time, and I asked who he was trying to contact. It is not mandatory for me to have this information, but I like to draw up a mental image before a session and meditate upon it. I find that there is a difference in the energy among spirits, depending upon gender or relationship to the sitter.

It was then that he informed me that the reading was for his wife, that she simply wanted a "spiritual reading." Because of the distance involved, I suggested that it might be better if they found a psychic reader in the Miami area. I was then told, rather sternly, "My wife has checked out your website, and has chosen you to do the reading. We will see you on Wednesday at 2:00 p.m."

When they arrived, they took a seat in my reading room. My immediate focus went to the man. I sensed his station in life, and stated, "You must be high up the ladder in what you do." He told me that he was a college professor in a high-profile military school.

I looked directly into the man's eyes and said, "You didn't tell me the truth about your purpose for coming here. The two of you want to contact your son who committed suicide. He is telling me that if I can't prove to you that it is him coming through, you will definitely leave. Your son is telling me, *Dad needed a new inverter for his motor home.*

The father looked at his wife in disbelief and said, "I took the motor home in for repair this past Monday. This morning, I received a call that the refrigerator and television were now running. All I needed was a new inverter"

We spent about an hour with many validations and messages coming through. Unfortunately, we had to end with an unpleasant message I had to give them from their son who told me, *The reason I took my life was because I felt I could never live up to dad's expectations.*

Normally when I see a cause of death, I would not be so direct. I would typically start with a checklist of questions leading up to the reason of death. I would try to be gentler with the delivery of the message. Their son, however, felt that he had many shortcomings while he was here. In effectively communicating to his parents that it was really him, he passed with flying color. I salute him for a job well done.

Censored

Spirits do not like to be "tested." In fact, they do censor information. A good friend of mine, Bob, came to me at a point when I had just become comfortable with giving individual readings. Because I was fairly new at this, I felt that I had to have music, darkened room, incense burning, and the whole ball of wax.

My first session with Bob lasted for three hours and netted just four validations from his brother. While I was disappointed with the results, Bob had come to the session hoping to receive any message at all from his brother. We agreed to give it another try in a few days.

The subsequent session was more successful and meaningful. Bob was hungry for more, more, more and kept coming back to me almost weekly.

His brother would unexpectedly give me messages when I was alone. I could be doing tasks such as mowing my yard, and he would come through telling me what Bob was doing at that very moment. Bob enjoyed this strange interaction.

Months after his first reading, Bob came to my house with a list of questions for his brother. The reading started off well. As Bob continued reading off from his list, several answers were given.

Then Bob asked, "Why are we really here?"

I clearly saw a woman's face, inches from my face. I saw her index finger cover her lips. She said the words, "You're asking too many questions."

I immediately snapped out of the reading. For a good month after that, my communication skills were shut down. I clearly got the message. Now when people cross that line, I inherently sense and respect that there are rules that we must follow. Spirits hold all the cards and have the answers, but in their wisdom, they do not always choose to give us everything.

Ray of Hope

Glenda, and her husband Richard, came to me for a reading. Richard appeared emaciated and told me that he was in the final stages of cancer. Richard's dad came through for him. The first validation was that of a strange concoction that dad used to make for him made of watermelon. Richard was extremely surprised that I could come up with such a statement.

I already knew that, while his wife was very open minded and enthusiastic about the reading, Richard was a skeptic. I made the statement to Richard, "You're afraid of sleeping bags?"

He replied that as a child, his friends zipped him inside a sleeping bag, and he thought he would die. He would never go near one again. There were many more accurate messages for Richard. We had a good dialogue about the other side and what it is like.

I shifted gears and felt very positive about his prognosis. I said, "Stay with the treatments, you're going to beat this."

Glenda told me that Richard had given up hope entirely. A short time later, I ran into her, and she thanked me for the reading. I asked how Richard was doing. She told me that he had died two weeks after the reading. I was confused and angry about the message of hope that I had been given for him. I did not understand why the spirits told me that he would beat cancer. Glenda informed me that the last weeks of his life were the best she had observed in over two years. She said that he was whistling, eating again, in an upbeat mood, and went peacefully in his sleep.

Spirits knew that my message of hope would give Richard and his family the comfort that they needed. Often spirit messages are not what we perceive them to be. They are not "black and white." In reality, Richard did "beat cancer" during his remaining days.

Glenda came to me for a reading six months later, and Richard came through with a message about spending time with her on the dock. Every night at sunset, Glenda would pray to him from her dock on the St Johns River. Richard wanted her to know that he was there with her.

Future Events

Is our future already planned? Gene and Arlene, friends from the north, were visiting me for a few weeks in June. Believe it or not, I am not always in the "spirit world." I try to act normal and have a good time, just like everybody else. As much as I love and appreciate my gift, it is healthy for me to take a break from it. I have my own life to live.

Just before dinner one evening, Arlene said, "Not now, but one day while I'm here, I'd like to have a reading. I'd love to hear from my mother and father."

I told her I would, but that I was now seeing her dad with two swollen feet.

"Oh My God, that's my dad," she yelled. She decided now was the time for the reading. It was like her mom and dad had been waiting for her to make the first move.

We went into the reading, and Arlene recognized many of the messages. However, one was a mystery to her. I clearly saw a calendar with the date "September 9" circled on it. She said that date meant nothing to her. I was emphatic that it was of importance.

When Arlene returned home to Rhode Island, she circled September 9 on her calendar. A few days before that date, she called me to tell me that a surprise retirement party had been planned for Gene on September 9. That date being circled on the calendar made it more difficult for Arlene to keep the secret.

The Cruise

I did a reading for a lady who had lost her husband during a cruise to Barbados. They had been on many cruises during their lifetime and, because of their ages, considered that this would be their last. When I started the reading, I saw a large ship out at sea fighting a terrible storm.

She said, "Yes, I understand." This had further, dramatic meaning, as she continued to tell me the story of their voyage. She started out emotionally, "The cruise ship had just left port and was just three hours out to sea. My husband entered the cabin in a happy mood, gave me a hug and kiss, and told me that this would be our best cruise ever. He went into the lavatory and suffered a massive heart attack. Emergency personnel transported him down to lower quarters. The medical attendants could not save him. I wanted to take my husband's body off the ship as soon as possible to our home town. The ship's captain told me that he had to consider all the other passengers and could not turn around. I had to endure seven days on the ship, knowing that my husband was on board with me, but I could not be with him."

Her husband did come through with many validations, but I felt this reading was more for her being able to tell the story of her trauma.

Special Delivery

Breaking the Code

Today's micro technology offers spirit a broader source of communication, while requiring less energy of them. I've experienced many and varied examples of this type of communication.

While doing a reading for a woman whose husband had passed, our phone call was interrupted by someone calling in to her number. She looked at the caller ID which displayed her deceased husband's name and cell phone number. Her husband's account had been deactivated a year earlier. She could see his phone lying on the counter with a dead battery. Since her husband's passing, his number had never come up on her phone. Why should it, since it had been cancelled.

Another high-tech message was delivered to a woman from her deceased husband. She contacted me for a reading, hoping to obtain his password from his computer, as they each had separate accounts on Windows XP. The husband took care of the checking account and other financial information. The reading was successful, but he gave no indication of the specific password.

The next morning, the woman powered up her computer and went into another room for coffee. When she returned and sat down to log in, to her amazement, her husband's account was open and ready for viewing. Though she did not get the password, she was able to transfer the relevant information to her account. Now why didn't he just give me, the medium, the password and make me look good? Again, it's their call.

Shining Star

Computers are a very effective means of communication for spirit – especially since we are all on them so much. I was helping a friend of mine, who had lost her 30-year-old son, compile pictures on the computer for a CD slide show at his memorial.

We were going through hundreds of pictures, choosing the right ones. When a picture of her son, her husband, and herself came up on the screen, a unique phenomenon occurred. From the bottom of the picture on the screen, a glowing shower of stars shot up through the picture to the top of the screen. They were majestic and unlike anything I had ever seen.

Karen, the mother, said, "How did you do that?"

I said, "I didn't do anything." That has never happened before."

We were both in awe as she told me, "I always referred to him as my "shining star." He was an ambitious young man and used to say, *I'm shooting for the stars.*"

Had I been working on the project alone and seen the stars, it wouldn't have had the same impact or significance. Sometime later, Karen remembered that her son had three stars tattooed on the upper portion of his back.

The Fan

Some spirits have more energy than others. I did a phone reading for Diane, whose deceased husband had been in law enforcement and had taken his own life. Bob did not come through with any messages for the first hour.

Diane then told me, "You won't believe this, the light on my ceiling fan is pulsing on and off slowly. I just walked under it, and the air is freezing cold. The light is brilliant blue. I know it is Bob."

After about ten minutes of her describing what was going on in the room, I asked if she had a video recorder.

She said, "Yes."

When she turned the recorder on, it said "no service." This is not a typical error message for a camcorder. She retrieved a second camcorder that she had recently purchased but had never used. Diane was able to record fifteen minutes of video that clearly showed an unexplainable blue light pulsing slowly on and off. The ceiling fan had a white globe light. The blue light was more of a narrow beam shooting vertically to the floor, similar to that of a laser.

My knowledge of electronics encouraged me to ask her specific questions. I asked if the light switch was a dimmer or a toggle switch.

"It's a toggle switch."

"How many lights are in the fan fixture?"

"There are three, small, clear bulbs. The outer light globe is a frosted white."

During giving me this information, Diane said, "Oh my God, I see my husband's silhouette; it's as if he's hanging from the fan."

I was intrigued and asked if she could send me a copy of the DVD. She said that she would.

Upon receiving the DVD, I studied her recording for potential flaws or manipulation. After watching it several times, I was left with no doubt that this was, in fact, her husband's spirit. We later tried for another reading, and he still would not come through. His preference of communication seemed to be through the metaphysical.

Subtle Signs

As with the fan above, not all messages are sent through high technology. After giving a reading to a woman for her deceased husband, she emailed me about a clock incident. She had a banjo clock that she wound once a week on Sunday. I had given her a reading on a Tuesday. She told me that she noticed at about 10:00 a.m. on the following Wednesday, after the reading, that her clock had stopped; the pendulum was still. The time on the clock read 11:59 from the night before. This was the exact time that her husband had passed six months earlier.

Typically after a reading, people are more cognizant of subtle signs from the spirit world. Many will report back to me after a reading that they had some type of connection with their loved ones. These messages may come through dreams, electronics, TVs, electrical devices, visions, smells or a keen sense of presence. Unfortunately, many people are programmed to not recognize them.

A friend told me that after losing her significant other, she wanted to totally clean the bedroom and bath they had shared. She had used lot of bleach and other strong cleaning products. She later walked back into the room and got the distinct aroma of chocolate chip cookies. She always said that her friend smelled like chocolate chip cookies.

Karen, who had recently lost her 30-year-old son, was gardening in her front yard. She had become accustomed to talking to her son whenever she was alone. She took off her gloves and went into the house. When she returned, her gloves were placed end to end, neatly, in an entirely different place. She totally believes that was a message from her son.

What's the Trick?

My older brother, Fred, had heard many stories from me about the spirit world, as I was developing my skills. He always kept his opinion to himself. I was quite surprised when he showed up at one of my large group readings.

I considered that it would be difficult for me to give him a reading because I grew up with him. I did the next best thing: I selected his wife for a reading. She lived and grew up in the Philippines. I had never met her parents. I brought through her dad and information about land development in the Philippines that could jeopardize his burial plot. My brother was surprised that I would have knowledge of this issue that had been such a concern to them.

I said, "Ouch. Your dad got shot through the leg."

My brother laughed and said, "No, he never got shot." His wife corrected him and stated that when her dad was much younger, a friend of his was cleaning a gun which fired, and the bullet went through her dad's leg.

The next day, around lunch time, I head the doorbell ring. To my surprise, my brother Fred was standing there. He came in and wanted to know the truth behind my psychic abilities. If it were a trick, he had to know.

When our mother passed, Fred could not acknowledge the reality of it. Knowing that my mom has helped me many times from the spirit world, I felt that she could bring healing to my brother, if he were open to it. To my total amazement, Fred asked if we could do a meditation. His timing was perfect.

I explained my techniques for doing meditation in a matter of minutes. I played quiet music, sat across from my brother, with eyes closed. Almost immediately, I saw a vision of our mother. Without moving her mouth, she spoke to me in sentences. She told me she was next going over to visit with Fred; that it would probably frighten him. She said she was going to hug and kiss him. I saw her turn and go over his way.

Within seconds, rather startled, Fred called out my name. I assured him that it was okay. I told him that mom had come to visit him and to simply enjoy what was about to happen.

I opened my eyes and saw Fred's head tilted back with a rapturous look on his face. After a couple of minutes, he jumped into an upright position and said, "I fell asleep, didn't I?"

I reminded Fred that when he had called my name, I told him that mom was with him. He still doubted that it was really mom.

I stated, "Mom was wearing a turquoise colored top with matching shorts." He looked puzzled and asked how I would know that, as he had just seen her in the same outfit.

Fred started to feel comfortable with the concept that he had reconnected with our mom. His hands were shaking as he demonstrated the way she had run her fingers through his hair. He said that he could really feel her touch. Fred is still very private with his thoughts regarding afterlife, but totally respects what I do.

The Importance of Meditation

Is the ability to communicate with spirits something that you are born with, or can it be learned? In my opinion, having a medium in the family tree is not a prerequisite for developing this ability. There are six children in my family, and I alone possess the gift. My sister has a strong desire to be able to connect with the other side but is not able to put her thoughts aside and hear messages of any kind.

For me, it was no walk in the park. I read every book I could find on the topic of mediumship and meditation. I attended many classes and groups that would meet for the sole purpose of being able to develop our intuitive skills and raise our vibration to a higher consciousness. Because energy tends to flow around the circle, the term sitting "in circle" is often used.

Depending on where you live, finding a meditation group may be difficult. Many new age bookstores carry fliers or have notices of classes being available locally. Such group meetings usually take place in a private residence and consist of a small number of people. Since these same people become familiar with each other, they may be hesitant to bring in a new member. Introducing a new personality will change the energy of the group; you may be invited in on a contingent basis. Any new person may present a positive, neutral, or negative source of energy to the gathering.

I have had it stressed upon me that spirit will keep an appointment once it is made. Meet at the same time every week! The good news is, a new person joining the group may see or hear messages on the first day. Others may take months before they are open enough to experience any message at all.

If you're going to form your own group, it's wise to select a teacher who is well established in the art of meditation. There is a trust factor invoked when you start climbing to higher planes. Someone must be cognizant of your physical body needs, as well as monitoring things such as facial expressions, to ensure that you are in a good place.

Once meditation has ended, there will be questions that only a seasoned instructor will be able to answer correctly. Learn from everyone's experiences. Personalities and egos will come into play. It is possible for two people to share the same meditation images and messages, especially when they are sitting directly across from each other. Some messages will not make sense at the time of the session but will have meaning by the time you return the following week.

You will not receive messages at every class. Keep an open mind and know that you are developing at your own pace. Many classes I attended were to simply de-stress my brain and soul. I noticed that I would open my eyes slowly after a meditation and my eyesight was sharper than normal. There was a rested feeling, as if waking from a nap. I could feel many thoughts waiting to enter my consciousness like water building up against a floodgate. With time, you learn to filter what you allow back in to your consciousness and to block out thoughts over which you have no control. As you may experience a real "high" after a meditation, you must use caution in performing everyday activities, such as driving.

I held a meditation with a lady friend of mine who had never done one before. We sat quietly for a time with soft music in the background. Afterwards, I said to my friend, "See if you can give me a reading."

She said, "I can't do that." She then said, "Do link sausages mean anything to you?"

I said, "Yes, my dad loved and made his own sausages."

"I see a dark-headed woman, a little heavy, twirling around in her apron and giving you a cute hello."

I knew that she was describing my mother. My friend was amazed that these images had come to her so readily, as neither of us had gotten any messages during the meditation. This was the very first time my friend had attempted to do a reading. Her brief success must have come from her concentration and open mindedness. It's always a treat for me to be on the receiving end.

Flying Around the Lake

I conducted another meditation with three friends. The one couple had lost their son in the last six months. We sat quietly, eyes closed, for about twenty minutes. I opened my eyes during the session and noticed that John's head was tilted back, with a smile on his face. We continued in silence for several more minutes. I asked each one if they had gotten anything.

They all said, "No."I was disappointed for them.

John hesitantly said, "Well, I flew around my lake."

I was startled and asked, "Why didn't you tell us?"

John said, "I thought I was dreaming." He further explained that he felt someone was with him, flying to his left. He said that it was a wonderful, floating feeling of freedom. He further elaborated, "We toured the lake three times."

"That was your son, John," I told him.

"It felt like my son, but I never saw him."

John told us that their son loved their lake, as they had so often boated and skied on it. After John revisited his so-called "dream," he could remember more details of his experience. He said that he really felt good that he had just spent time with his son.

John's wife later told me that this meditation, and message for John, had helped him more than anything prior in dealing with the loss of their son.

If you have never tried a meditation, I encourage you to do so. A meditation gives your brain a chance to rest and reboot. When we are asleep, our body is at rest, but the brain is still active. A conscientious time-out gives you a chance to recharge and clean out the clutter your brain has stored.

Animals in Spirit

Rainbow Bridge

*J*ust this side of Heaven is a place called Rainbow Bridge...
When an animal dies that has been especially close to someone here, that pet goes to Rainbow Bridge. There are meadows and hills for all of our special friends so they can run and play together. There is plenty of food and water and sunshine, and our friends are warm and comfortable. All the animals that had been ill and old are restored to health and vigor; those who were hurt or maimed are made whole and strong again, just as we remember them in our dreams of days and times gone by.

The animals are happy and content, except for one small thing: they miss someone very special to them; who had to be left behind. They all run and play together, but the day comes when one suddenly stops and looks into the distance. The bright eyes are intent; the eager body quivers. Suddenly he begins to break away from the group, flying over the green grass, his legs carrying him faster and faster. YOU have been spotted, and when you and your special friend finally meet, you cling together in joyous reunion, never to be parted again. The happy kisses rain upon your face; your hands again caress the beloved head, and you look once more into the trusting eyes of your pet, so long gone from your life but never absent from your heart.

Then you cross Rainbow Bridge together…
Author unknown…

Mr. Ed the Talking Horse

People are often surprised during a reading when their pets come through and indicate that they are with a loved one. Some will show their color, breed, size and even give their nickname. The messages are typically brief but have real significance to the sitter.

Do pets communicate with us mentally when they are here? When I first moved to Florida I went to Clay Maverick's riding club with family. Tracey, a good friend, was frustrated with the behavior of her horse, Stretch. She asked me if I could spend some time with him and intuitively connect with him to figure out his problem. Horses were foreign to me at that time. I found their size to be rather intimidating. Stretch stood before me, a halter around his head, with a lead line connected. I walked him away from the other people and horses. As I led this mammoth animal away, I had no idea what his problems were or how I was supposed to help.

Within minutes, I heard, in a voice that sounded like Mister Ed the talking horse, say, "I know, I'm in trouble for biting, biting, biting."

I thought, "Horses can bite? Why am I so close to one?" I decided to answer back using mental telepathy, a technique used when communicating with spirits.

"Your master is going to send you to a new home, and it may not be as good as the one you have now. Why are you acting out?"

"I don't know where I fit," Stretch answered. He showed me a scene in which his mother died giving birth to him. He added, "I get scared when I hear big motors."

As I returned to Tracey, passing her the lead line, I noticed several people watching in anticipation of what Stretch would do next.

"We were waiting for Stretch to buck and do his thing with you," Tracey said. "Did you give him a tranquilizer? He has never looked so calm."

I asked the question about Stretch's mother dying while giving birth to him. If this were a true statement, it would mean that a horse had just talked to me, and I was able to hear it!

"Yes, Tracey said. How would you know that?"

"He told me about it, and he also said that something happened when she died that had made him afraid of loud motors."

Tracey told me that she was there when Stretch was born, and that after the mother had died, a tractor removed her body from the stall. "There are many trucks with loud motors at the horse club, and they frighten Stretch," I let her know. "He wants you to spend more time with him. He thinks of you as his mom."

Tracey admitted that she had been busy and neglectful of brushing and spending time with Stretch. Before the night was over, several people wanted a "horse reading," and I had to explain that I typically don't do that type of reading.

Later, I bought a horse and learned to "Barrel Race". The bond and connection between rider and his horse is amazing. Riding in the saddle can feel like all fifteen hundred pounds of muscle are part of you. My horse and I had great respect for each other, but he never connected to me telepathically. I always sent him kind messages, hoping that he would receive them.

Jack Ass

I had another horse experience. My niece, Donna, and her husband, Rob, were visiting me and were in a glum mood because they had lost their horse, Louie, two days earlier. Donna was curious to see if he could come through in spirit. She asked me if Louie had to be on the other side for a certain length of time in order to come through.

I told her what I have experienced: "Spirits can visit with living people as soon as they cross over. Many people report "knowing" when a friend or relative has passed, even though they may be miles apart."

I was surprised when I saw an image of a bucket of water being poured onto a pile of hay. Donna let me know that her horse had severe allergy problems and that she had been required to pour water onto his hay. I then heard the horse give me a strange, high-pitched whistle like that of a jack ass. I asked Donna if she could relate to that.

She said, "No."

Rob spoke up and stated that he fed the horses every morning after Donna went to work. When approaching them, he would give a shrill whistle, like that of a braying donkey.

"That's the first time I've heard that," Donna said.

Rob then mimicked the donkey bray, as he did every morning. This gave Donna a confidence level that her horse was, indeed, okay.

On Thin Ice

Christine came to me for a reading a few months after her fiancé, Rick, died while on a hiking trip in the mountains of New Hampshire. They had hiked all day and were resting near a frozen stream with their dog Boomer. The dog was playing on the frozen stream when he fell through the ice. Rick made several attempts to rescue him from the shore. As a last resort, he walked out onto the ice which plunged him into freezing water. The current pulled him under the ice and out of sight. Boomer somehow made it back to dry land unscathed.

Christine's only option to get help was to retreat to the base of the mountain and contact the rangers. She hiked the forty-five minute trail back to the ranger station. When she arrived, she was told that the mishap had already been reported. The rangers said that a search party was on the way to the scene.

Christine traveled home that night and anxiously awaited any news about Rick. When she had heard nothing for several days, she called to see if the search party had any information. She was told that the body had been found. However, it wasn't Rick. Apparently, the same day, another body had fallen through the ice in a nearby location. Because of the confusion, the rangers formed another search party, and Rick's body was found downstream a few days later.

During the reading, Rick came through with accurate validations for Christine. He let her know that she did the right thing in leaving and seeking help from the rangers. She had been blaming herself for not, also, going out onto the ice to try to help.

This was an extremely sad story, and I know the messages served to comfort Christine. It, once again, emphasizes the fragility of life.

Snowball

I was doing a group reading in Philadelphia, and a man sitting in the front row was giving off rather negative vibes. His arms were crossed, and he was sinking down into his seat. "I take it you don't believe in this stuff?" I said to him.

"Nope," was his reply.

"Your wife talked you into coming here today, is this correct?"

"Yep," another to-the-point answer.

"Your dad, in spirit, tells me that he is taking good care of Snowball. Who is Snowball?"

The man sat up straight and unfolded his arms. With tears running down his face, he said, "I'm a K-9 officer here in Philly, and my dog, Snowball, was shot and died a few months ago."

"Your dad is not happy with you," I stated. "What did you do with his matchbook, collection?"

He replied, "My dad traveled the world and he would collect matchbooks whenever possible. This week, my son and I packed up his collection and put it in the attic."

"Nope," I said, "Dad wants you to put his collection back where it was or things are going to fly"!

Name That Pet

I did an in-house reading for a woman and her two daughters. Their hope was that the woman's parents would come in, which they did. As we were wrapping up the session, I noticed one of the girls whispering to her mother.

I asked, "Is there a problem?"

I heard the mother say to her daughter, "He doesn't do that."

"Do what?" I asked.

The mother replied, "We lost a pet two weeks ago and we were hoping that you would be able to connect with it."

"Was it a he?"

"Yes."

In disbelief, I had to say to them, "He's telling me that Mexican blood runs through his veins."

They exploded with laughter. "Yes, he was a Mexican Chihuahua. We even spoke to him in Spanish."

Chablis

A close friend of mine, Sharon, went to see a medium while she was in Sedona, Arizona. She had never been to one before and was selecting from bios posted on the wall at an artists' village. She chose "Scotty Littlestar," loving the name.

After being seated in front of Scotty, Sharon removed her shoes and jewelry. Scotty looked over Sharon's shoulder and said, "Someone is here with you." Sharon was a bit puzzled; she had not recently lost a close loved one.

Scotty elaborated, "I see a large, white dog; it appears to be shaking off drops of water, which seems strange. I think it's a Poodle or Poodle blend. I can't make out the name, but it is very unusual."

Sharon began to cry, as she knew immediately that the dog was her beloved white Standard Poodle, "Chablis," who had died two years earlier. Chablis had grown up on the beach on Little Gasparilla Island in Florida. She was a natural in the water.

Scotty said, "She's growling at me, protecting you, and doesn't seem to want me to get too close. That dog is always with you."

Scotty gave Sharon other validations, but the one most important to her was the message from Chablis. She knew that Chablis was okay and still around her. This was Sharon's first real experience with the spirit world, and she will always cherish her trip to Sedona.

Her first reading with Scotty was an eye-opener, as what she had expected to receive was to have her fortune told.

I have since worked with Sharon in giving messages from her loved ones. Her first visit to Sedona opened the doors for greater spiritual experiences and understanding. The more we experience, the more we understand.

My Wish for You

My life has been, and is now, constantly evolving. I find that I must keep a delicate balance between the life I am living here on earth and dealing with the elements of the spirit world. My mission, through spirit messages, is to bring peace and comfort to others. It is also to assure that there is, indeed, another life after this one.

I hope that through these true stories, you gain a greater understanding of what we often consider a mystery or falsehood. That being evidence of an afterlife.

Hopefully these messages have helped to alleviate the fear of death in knowing that there is love and forgiveness for all; that our loved ones are around us and are okay.

Searching for the truth is a common quest for man. Through my experiences, may you open your hearts and minds to the infinite possibilities that exist in this realm and other spheres.

May God bless you and your loved ones,
Chuck

Website: www.chuckbergman.com